Whack-a-Mole

THE PRICE WE PAY
FOR EXPECTING PERFECTION

David Marx

By Your Side Studios
6900 N Dallas Pkwy, Suite 750
Plano, TX 75024
www.byyoursidestudios.com
www.whackamolethebook.com

First Edition: August 2009

Library of Congress Control Number: 2009924849
Marx, David
Whack-a-mole

ISBN-10: 0-615-28307-1
ISBN-13: 978-0-615-28307-4

For my wife, Dawne,
and our five children—for you, I live.

For the one in 21—for you, I write.

Table of Contents

Prologue

Whack-a-Mole.

It's an arcade game. It's an online game. It's at many a local pizza parlor. Kids love it. Watching moles pop up, the child with a hammer in hand seeks to hit the exposed mole before it retreats back into the safety of its hole.

Whack-a-Mole is also a metaphor for modern life. It's a game we play with each other—particularly here in the U.S. It's how we respond to predictable human fallibility. It's how we set expectations of each other, how we respond when our fellow human being makes a mistake. Whack-a-Mole.

We play the game at home—with our spouses when they forget to stop at the store on the way home from the office and with our kids when they spill their milk at the dinner table. We play the game at work, writing corporate disciplinary policies that literally outlaw human error. Our legislators are good at the game, too, writing laws that make human error a felony punishable by years in prison.

The mole in these examples is the adverse event, those outcomes in life that just don't seem to be what we wanted.

They're created most often by the mistakes we make, missing that stop sign seemingly hidden behind an old elm tree, addressing that sensitive e-mail to the wrong person, forgetting that the gas nozzle is still connected to the car when we pull away from the gas pump. In the aftermath of these mistakes, both catastrophic and relatively benign, we take the easy route: How bad was the harm? Who touched it last? Who is to blame? Who is to pay? As adults, we push our need for "justice" to the point that every adverse outcome in life must have an accompanying blameworthy human behind it. It's the game of Whack-a-Mole.

It's a game that costs us dearly. We're all poised to pounce, caught up in the adult version of Whack-a-Mole, with the media all too willing to help swing the hammer even before the investigation has started. Bad outcome must mean bad actor. Whack that bad actor and the game is won.

This book argues that our Whack-a-Mole approach to inevitable and often predictable human error is ineffective, inefficient, and unjust; it does nothing to enable us to learn what we might do differently next time, or what systems we might put in place to minimize the chances of causing the same adverse outcome again.

The statistics are these. You have a one-in-21 chance of dying from accidental causes in your life. That's a one in 1,600 chance of accidental death per year. It's a one in 584,000 chance you will accidentally die today, all things being equal.

The greatest threat to your inadvertent demise is a medical mistake—one of our hard working doctors, nurses, or pharmacists making a mistake. Some reports say medical errors lead to 200,000 lives lost per year in the U.S. alone. Consider this: for every one person who dies in war, four will die in automobile accidents. And for every person in the U.S. who dies in an automobile accident, four to five will die from a preventable medical mistake. Nowhere in life's endeavors does our human fallibility lead to so much harm.

On January 25, 2000, Dr. Lucian Leape, a Harvard professor of health, testified before Congress on what he saw as the state of healthcare safety in the U.S. He told Congress that the single greatest impediment to error prevention in the medical industry is that "we punish people for making mistakes." A co-author of the Institute of Medicine's (IOM) report, *To Err is Human*, Leape cited that study's estimated 44,000 to 98,000 annual deaths that are caused as a result of medical error alone. He said that healthcare providers would often only report what they could not hide. The process is simple: doctors make mistakes, professional boards take licensing action, and newspapers demonize the dedicated professional who made the mistakes. Case closed. Problem solved. Mole whacked—although we haven't learned anything about what we can do better.

This book is about justice at the interpersonal level between spouses, kids, and neighbors; at the organizational level between supervisors, employees and coworkers; and at a societal level in the expectations we set for each other. Yes, we must cast a net to find and address behaviors that do not conform to familial, organizational, or societal values and expectations. Yes, we have a need to hold each other

3

appropriately accountable. Yet when we cast that net today in search of wrongdoers, we cast it so wide that it catches mere fallible human beings, branding them as either a naughty child, a bad spouse, an incompetent driver, or a bad employee. Even our criminal net has been cast so far as to catch human beings who had absolutely no intention of causing harm; yet, we label them criminal just the same. It's Whack-a-Mole.

It's a game that has a very insidious flip side. While we've learned in the game to lie in wait for the adverse event to pop up, ready to strike when we see the harm occur, we have largely given up on accountability for our personal choices. The game has made our performance all about the outcome. It's called "no harm, no foul." We turn a blind eye to those imposing unnecessary risk, so long as the outcome is good. It's Kiefer Sutherland's character, Jack Bauer, in the hit show 24. Jack Bauer breaks any rule he feels he needs to, so long as the end justifies the means. It's yet another aspect of Whack-a-Mole.

There is a better way, as the stories that follow will show. Whack-a-Mole may be addicting for its simplicity, but it's not a productive way to deal with adverse events. Whether it's our attitude toward spilt milk at the dinner table or our attitude toward the airline pilot who misses an item on a checklist, we simply cannot believe that an expectation of perfection will get us the results we want. We spend far too much time looking at the severity of the adverse outcome (how bad was it?) and who was the unfortunate soul to be closest to the harm. In turn, we spend far too little time addressing the system design that got us there and the behavioral choices of the humans in those systems that might have ultimately contributed to the adverse outcome. It's called Whack-a-Mole.

PART ONE

The Basic Problem

We live in a world that demands perfection. Unfortunately, we're inherently fallible human beings. We are going to hurt each other—it's a fact of life, a cost of doing business. On the bright side, we can reduce the odds.

A Date Gone Awry

September 25, 2005. My wife and I had plans to celebrate the twenty-third anniversary of our first date. Because we were married on December 22, our wedding anniversary falls within a whirlwind of holiday activity. The end of September makes for a much more relaxed, enjoyable time to celebrate.

My wife planned this date. She picked a small restaurant in our town, an old house that had been converted to a restaurant, reminiscent of our favorite restaurant near campus where we met twenty-three years earlier. She had even delivered rose petals to the restaurant earlier in the day so that they would be scattered on the table when we arrived. She had planned the perfect evening and was hoping for a little perfection in the way it played out.

I had a simple task: Get ready. No work. Just be prepared to leave the house by 7:00 p.m. The important sequence of events that ultimately made the date go awry started a few hours earlier when I hopped into the shower. I had noticed a developing rash on my leg and it was beginning to itch. It looked and felt like I had touched something that ought to have been avoided. Not poison ivy, but something a bit milder. On this important night, though, I was determined not to let a simple rash bother me all evening. I diagnosed it as an allergic reaction and headed off to find the suitable pharmacological remedy in our medicine cabinet, tucked safely out of the reach of our five children. Knowledgeable on the proper use of all these pills, sprays, and lotions, I, as an adult, knew what and how much to use, and I knew exactly what I needed. Benadryl. Two pills would do the trick.

We arrived at the restaurant anticipating great food and jazz music on the patio after our meal. Along with the flowers at the table, the proprietors toasted us with two glasses of champagne as we entered the restaurant. The evening had started well.

About an hour into the date, around the completion of my New York steak and half a bottle of Cabernet Sauvignon, something happened. Well, my wife could see that something had happened. Gazing across the table at me, she discovered that I was asleep. Though I cannot recall how my wife woke me, I do recall what she said—something about how had she not been in love with me for the past twenty-plus years, she would have taken considerable offense at my behavior! Our expectations for a perfect evening were beginning to slip...

As I struggled to wake up, I remember saying something like, "I don't know what's going on. I just can't stay awake." Now, with more mental acuity, I would have recognized the potential risk in this statement; my wife might infer that I thought she had become so boring after twenty-three years together that I was unable to stay awake for our anniversary celebration. Nothing could have been further from the truth; it just came out that way.

In retrospect, I can easily imagine what my wife had experienced. At 8:30 p.m., during a romantic dinner, her husband had fallen asleep in the middle of a restaurant. In college, when I was courting her, it was a much different story. We both worked in the restaurant industry and were often up past 2:00 a.m. Sometimes we'd head to our local Denny's, or if we were feeling particularly adventuresome, we'd make the hour and a half trip to Tucson on my motorcycle for breakfast after closing down our restaurants. Back then, we had stamina. In my thirties, I began to fade— having entered the corporate world, I was exhausted by the time I arrived home. A late night was 11:00 p.m., sometimes 10:00 p.m.

Now here I was in my mid-forties, struggling to stay awake past 8:00 p.m. My lovely wife could only wonder about the day I would not wake up at all. Based on the abrupt ending to our meal, it was looking like that morning could come by my mid-sixties. Rather than die from disease or folly, I would die by simply not waking up. While I could think of nothing but sleep, my wife was still thinking about the rest of the evening she had planned. Jazz on the patio. Time together *sans* children—with me awake.

While there was surely a cause to my abnormal desire to sleep, that was not what my wife was chasing. Her concern was more along the lines of accountability. Put simply: how could I atone for this sin? What price would I pay for spoiling a well-planned, wonderful evening? I just wanted to go home, climb in bed and sleep off the evening as a bad memory. My wife was not going to have any part of that. Too much thought and effort had been poured into this evening. At this point, she became quite directive, instructing me to proceed with her to the patio where we would sit and listen to the jazz musicians, for at least two songs. Blame had been assigned and disciplinary action taken.

Benadryl labels are straightforward. Most contain verbiage that communicates a message such as, "May cause drowsiness. Do not take with alcohol." How could I have missed this crucial piece of information? Easy. I have a Y-chromosome. *Ergo*, I did not read the label. To me, Benadryl was like aspirin and I knew, or thought I knew, when I should take each. Aspirin for headaches. Benadryl for allergic reactions. Who needed directions? Me.

The Benadryl reacted with the champagne and wine, directly resulting in an impromptu naptime. My wife had planned the night in perfect detail. She was dressed to perfection. The rose petals scattered on the table made the date look like something out of a Cinderella story. My wife had done everything to create a perfect evening with her husband. The one thing out of her control was me. I took Benadryl without thinking about the side effects.

Adverse drug event—that's what healthcare providers call it. Mine was relatively benign; it resulted in one disastrous date. But in the hectic, fast-paced world of healthcare, thousands of patients suffer from adverse drug events every day. Some of these events are simply the statistically predictable side effects of the drug/human interaction. Others, however, are the result of error.

Human error. Your doctor may write down the wrong drug or the wrong dose. She might write the order for the wrong patient. A pharmacist might make the medication mistake and dispense the wrong drug or dose. Nurses can draw up the incorrect dosage into a syringe or deliver the medication to the wrong patient. Or it may be the patient who does not read the medication label, or even after looking at the instructions, makes a simple measurement mistake that leads to the adverse drug event.

The healthcare industry refers to those events involving human error as "medication errors." They occur every day around the world. In some cases, patients and their doctors will never know they've experienced a medication error due to the body's ability to adjust to the unintended drug or dose. In other cases, it may mean an extended hospital stay to correct this new healthcare-caused condition. In the worst cases, the patient dies as a result.

The quandary facing the healthcare industry is the same one my wife faced after our disastrous date. What do we do when things go awry? We face a two-fold challenge: 1) hold those who caused the event appropriately accountable, and 2) make fixes to prevent future events. What we will see is that these two goals are often at odds with each other. And when Whack-a-Mole rules the day, the prevention of future events takes a back seat. As Lucian Leape said, the single greatest impediment to safety is that we punish people for making mistakes. In healthcare today, as with any industry, from aviation to children's day care, potential responses to the individual who makes the mistake run the gamut from termination to license revocation, from criminal indictment to civil lawsuit.

Whack-a-Mole.

Spinning the Roulette Wheel

There she sat, January 28, 1986, on the pad awaiting the countdown for the launch of the space shuttle *Challenger*'s Mission STS-51L. Four million pounds of thrust were about to hurl her and six astronauts into space on what were, essentially, two Roman candles. By the time they clear the pad, they're traveling at 100 miles per hour. Once they reach orbit, they'll float through the atmosphere at about 17,500 miles per hour—all inside an aluminum aircraft coated with fragile foam held on by glue. Seventy-three seconds after lift-off Christa Corrigan McAuliffe was dead, the *Challenger* having exploded over the Atlantic in front of a gathered crowd filled with her students and family members.

Among approximately 10,000 applicants, McAuliffe was selected to be the first non-scientist in space. A gifted teacher, McAuliffe taught social studies, history and economics at Concord High School in Framingham, Massachusetts. Often relying on guest speakers and field trips to bring her subjects to life for her students, McAuliffe was looking forward to the two on-board lessons she was scheduled to teach (arguably the greatest field trip any teacher has ever organized).

Instead, an O-ring on the right solid rocket booster failed, starting a chain reaction of spilled fuel, structural failure of the external fuel tank, a massive explosion and finally, the crew compartment, the solid rocket boosters and the rest of the spacecraft, crashing into the ocean. To this day, it is not clear whether the crew died as the *Challenger* broke apart or whether they died on impact with the Atlantic Ocean.

There are two general views one can have toward the inherent risks we face in life. One is hopeful—if everyone obeys the rules, all will be well. The other is perhaps pessimistic: risk is everywhere and it's just a matter of time until I get taken out. I consider the first view as profoundly naïve and the latter as profoundly realistic.

Consider a space shuttle astronaut. He might reasonably believe that it's going to be a great day, so long as everyone does his or her job error-free. There is no risk that cannot be eliminated by good, roll-up-your-sleeves engineering and professional, hard-working technicians. Or, being aware of space shuttle design reliability, an astronaut might just as reasonably think of life like a roulette wheel. Every day is a spin of the wheel.

The roulette wheel has thirty-six spots, plus a zero and a double zero. Half of the thirty-six numbered spots are red, half black. You can bet on a number, a group of numbers, a color, or you can place a bet on either of two green spots, the zero or double zero. You place your bets, spin the wheel, and hope that the ball falls into the spot you've bet on. It's gambling. Win big, lose big.

So what makes life like the spinning of a roulette wheel? It's this: you try to design the best systems around you, try to make the best choices you can, and then, well, you spin the wheel. The inherent risks of life cannot be eliminated; they are always there. You cannot know which horse is going to win the Kentucky Derby, and you cannot be guaranteed that you are going to get home this evening without being involved in a fatal car accident. You do have control, but it has its limits.

Christa McAuliffe's space shuttle was never designed to be perfect—not even close. At least one design risk assessment put loss of the space shuttle, principally on takeoff, at one catastrophic accident in every 212 missions. And that's not including any human error or more blameworthy human behavior. It's simply the risk of catastrophic equipment failure. Flying the space shuttle is not a risk-free endeavor. It was never meant to be. It is instead, for every astronaut, the spin of a roulette wheel with at most 212 spaces, where landing on double zero means the loss of your life.

Mission STS-51L was the twenty-fifth flight of a shuttle into orbit. On this cold January day, NASA spun the roulette wheel and the ball dropped into the double zero spot. But that's not the view most of us took nor the view we read about in the papers or heard on the evening news. Many of us took the position that accidents like this should not happen; something must have gone wrong. Someone must be to blame. And as the accident investigation found, many things did go terribly wrong. The point is, however, that even if there had been no defective O-ring, even if there had been no risky pre-launch decisions, there would still have been a one in 212 chance of a catastrophic event. The space shuttle mission, like every endeavor in life, was not risk-free.

The "if we all just do our jobs correctly, if we all just follow the rules" club sees the bad outcome as a blameworthy incident because nothing happens by accident. If there is an adverse event, someone, some process, or some organization is to blame. That's where we stood in the days after the *Challenger* accident, standing in judgment, looking for whom to blame. After all, if people would just do what they are supposed to do, these things would not happen. Reporters, as a group, are naturally aligned to this view of the world. "S**t Happens" never makes for a good headline. Bad outcomes must be caused by bad actors—that's the rule. The other view accepts that we humans are fallible, and that Mother Nature is sometimes harsh. In this view, adverse outcomes are not necessarily proof of a blameworthy actor, an evil corporate empire, or an out-of-control space agency. No matter how hard we try, every human endeavor has risk. In fact, for our astronauts on the pad today, their roulette wheel has been reduced from 212 spots to what seems to be 57 spaces. In the first 113 space shuttle missions, two have ended in catastrophic failure.

We wake up every morning knowing that it may be our last. Pessimistic? Yes. The hope comes in our ability to impact the odds. We do everything we can to make it safe— put on seatbelts, read the labels on medications, turn pan handles toward the back of the stove. Yet, after we've made all these efforts to reduce the risks that surround us, we must know that we have not reduced the risk to zero. We are stuck with our inherent, inescapable human fallibility. This view of life as a roulette wheel doesn't bother me. It's life. I know that a neighbor, distracted by his two children fighting in the back seat, might run a red light and hit me in the intersection. I know that the neighbor could be me, distracted by two of my five children fighting, who causes someone else's early demise. I know that my doctor may prescribe the wrong medication and that I might not catch the error. I know that my airline pilot might miss his approach and run our airplane aground short of the runway. I know much of this can occur without any evil intent, without any risky behavioral choices, without anything to blame other than simple human fallibility. Each day, I wake up to a certain number of spots on my roulette wheel with some chance of landing on double zero; this doesn't make me anxious, it makes me cherish each day.

PART TWO

OUR PREDICTABLE
HUMAN FALLIBILITY

We are all fallible human beings. We live in an inherently risky world where we create risk and cause undesirable outcomes. Whether you are a parent, a corporate CEO, a nuclear power plant operator, or a hedge fund manager, we all have to find a system of justice that balances the needs of an open learning environment, with the need to be "just"—to hold our children, our staff, and ourselves accountable for our actions. Part Two explores our different types of human fallibility, how our current culture reacts to this fallibility, and offers a proposal for a more supportive view.

To Err is Human

Because his wife had a late start to the day, Jim volunteered to take their eight-month-old son, Andrew, to daycare. This wasn't the typical routine—his wife usually swings by on her way to the bank where she works as an accountant. Jim, a manager at the local auto dealership, didn't mind the addition to his morning commute. As he drove toward the daycare center, with young Andrew sound asleep in the backseat of the family minivan, Jim received a call from an angry customer. Trying to calm the customer down, Jim stayed on the phone until he walked through the showroom doors. Unfortunately, the distracting phone call caused Jim to forget about daycare, leaving young Andrew soundly sleeping in the backseat of the minivan on an already warm day.

At this point, you might fill in the rest of the story one of two ways. Either someone observes that Andrew is sleeping in the increasingly hot minivan, or Jim finds his forgotten son when he leaves for home at the end of the day. For approximately forty-five people in the U.S. every year, this scenario turns tragic. We look in as observers, parents in particular, facing one of our worst nightmares. Many of us who have children have had close calls—forgetting to pick up our child at daycare, forgetting to bring him in the house when we arrive home.

So how do we describe this event? Adverse event? Mishap? Close call? Human error? It should be a given in our analysis that Jim did not want this to happen. Here we simply have a human error. There was no choice on Jim's part to cause harm or put his son in jeopardy. There was only a choice to take his child to daycare on the way to work. Short of any suspicious choices to be discussed in the next chapter, we would merely refer to this as human error. Terms like inadvertent and unintentional apply.

Statistics show that greater than 70 percent of aircraft accidents are caused by human error; this is the type of behavior to which those statistics refer. Good people making mistakes. Inadvertent actions and lack of intent abound. The safety sciences have known for years that it's possible to set up humans to make mistakes, even when it seems obvious that a human should be able to get it right. We generally cannot preclude the error, but we can influence its rate. Consider the simple test that follows on the next page. Your task is to count the number of times the letter "E" appears in the paragraph. A simple task, no trickery. Just count how many times you find the letter "E." I'll even give you a tip: there are more than 75, less than 100. So, start at the beginning and walk your way through the paragraph, counting as you go. How many E's do you count?

FRED IS A NURSE. FRED IS FEARFUL THAT HE MIGHT ERR IN HIS FIELD OF WORK, AND SUBSEQUENTLY FEELS THE HAMMER OF THE LAW FOR HIS FAILURE TO CONFORM TO HIS FIELD'S DUTY OF CARE. YOU EXPLAIN THAT THE PURPOSE OF NEGLIGENCE LAW IS TO ENSURE THAT AGGRIEVED PARTIES ARE MADE WHOLE BY MAKING THE PERSON WHO ERRS PAY FOR THE DAMAGES. IN FRED'S CASE, FRED WORKS FOR A HOSPITAL SYSTEM THAT MUST CARRY THE BURDEN FOR HIS ERROR. YOU FURTHER EXPLAIN TO FRED THAT IN THE CRIMINAL LAW, NEGLIGENCE HAS NOT GENERALLY BEEN CONSIDERED A CRIME BECAUSE NEGLIGENCE DID NOT HAVE THE REQUIRED MENS REA, OR "EVIL MIND." TODAY, HOWEVER, WE HOLD INDIVIDUALS ACCOUNT- ABLE FOR THEIR ERRORS BECAUSE THE PUBLIC SHOULD EXPECT NOTHING LESS FROM A HIGHLY TRAINED NURSE. AFTER ALL, EVERYONE SHOULD BE ABLE TO PERFORM FLAWLESSLY.

So what did you get? I have used this test in conferences across industries, with thousands of participants. Perhaps five percent of the participants get it right. Most will miss three to five of the E's. When allowed to count a second time, we still see a very high rate of error. Some will strangely count more E's than are present. We ask astronauts to fly to the Moon and Mars. We ask surgeons to perform complex surgery. Yet, when put to the test, we have trouble counting fewer than 100 identical letters within a paragraph.

Should we take this to mean we're all unintelligent or unprofessional, or perhaps just too lazy to give it our full effort? No. It simply demonstrates our human fallibility—even in the face of a relatively simple task of little consequence. We are not perfect machines. Our computer, on the other hand, can tell us within a split second how many E's are in the paragraph.

What we know from the study of human performance is that we can manipulate the display of information in ways that impact the rate of human error. If the anxiety-inducing view says that human error is inevitable, that each day of our lives is just a spin of the roulette wheel, we should all be comforted by the fact that we can control the rate of error through the systems we design and the choices we make within those systems. Consider the same paragraph below, just formatted a bit differently. What count do you now get with this paragraph?

Fred is a nurse. Fred is fearful that he might err in his field of work and subsequently feel the hammer of the law for his failure to conform to his field's duty of care. You explain that the purpose of negligence law is to ensure that aggrieved parties are made whole by making the person who errs pay for the damages. In Fred's case, Fred works for a hospital system that must carry the burden for his error. You further explain to Fred that in the criminal law, negligence has not generally been considered a crime because negligence did not have the required mens rea, or "evil mind." Today, however, we hold individuals accountable for their errors because the public should expect nothing less from a highly trained nurse. After all, everyone should be able to perform flawlessly.

Did you come up with a different number? If you are like most, you probably found a few instances that you did not see before. They were present in the first paragraph, just as they are here in this paragraph—even in the same place! In our desire to create the most reliable system for counting E's, we chose to discontinue the use of all capital letters, and to bold and italicize all the E's. The sciences, and common sense, can explain the improved accuracy, yet the obligation to count the letter was the same in both cases. In this reading, you should have come closer to counting the actual ninety-one occurrences of the letter "E." When should we be able to expect that a fellow human being will get it exactly right? Is a doctor or nurse allowed to miscount? An astronaut or pilot? A child trying his best on his homework?

In commercial aviation, we want to lower the rate of error, or at least mitigate its effects. Engineers use terms like barriers, recovery, and redundancy to describe the strategies to control the likelihood and impact of individual human mistakes. We do it for our safety. In contrast, when designing a game or sport, we might want to design in more opportunities for error, to drive differences between weaker and stronger performances. In sports, we seek to instill competition with rates of human error making the difference between winners and losers. The point is that we can control the rate of human error by how we design the system: the equipment we use, the procedures we follow, and the environment in which we work. We can raise or lower the error rate to meet system objectives (but still, the system will never be perfect).

So what should our framework of justice look like when we are asked to stand in judgment of our fellow human being after he or she has made a mistake? In sports, we expect that the error will be counted against the player. That's the point. The team that makes fewer errors generally wins the game. In the game of life, however, should the person who makes the error be viewed as the guy who lost the game? Should the nurse who makes a mistake be charged as a criminal and sent to prison?

We human beings are fallible creatures. When it comes to "E" counting, we do not have the reliability or precision of our home computer. What we do have, however, is a brain, and our home computer can only attempt to simulate it. Our brains may be flawed, but they are capable of many things a computer is not. We can love. That alone should make being born a human a better choice than being a computer. We as humans can do things that draw on context the way a computer cannot—at least with today's technology. Consider the paragraph below, something that's been kicked around the internet for years:

Aoccdrnig to a rscheearch at Cmabrigde Uinervtisy, it deosn't mttaer in waht oredr the ltteers in a wrod are, the olny iprmoetnt tihng is taht the frist and lsat ltteer be at the rghit pclae. The rset can be a total mses and you can sitll raed it wouthit prboelm. Tihs is bcuseae the huamn mnid deos not raed ervey lteter by istlef, but the wrod as a wlohe.

In reading this paragraph, we amaze ourselves at what we're able to pick up. We can read this seemingly unintelligible paragraph just about as fast as a paragraph written correctly. So much for teaching our kids the importance of proper spelling! Get only a few letters right and it seems that we are able to communicate just fine. We are impressive creatures, better equipped than the best of computers. But only in some tasks. We can't solve a mathematical equation as fast as a computer, and we make many more mistakes. When comparing computers to humans, there are some tasks where the computer is simply the better choice.

Helping the human succeed is the first task, and determining the appropriate course of action when they do not is the second task. How do we design good systems around predictably fallible humans? How do we view the mistake in hindsight, after it has happened?

In the Benadryl mishap, I had long grown complacent in reading the warnings on medications that I thought I understood. I had the ability to control my rate of error through the choices I made ahead of the date. Had I read the label, I would have likely chosen the rash over falling asleep during a much-anticipated dinner with my wife. So what did I do in response to my error? I learned. My wife, well, she helped. She was warm and compassionate when she saw I had fallen asleep. She only made me listen to two songs on the patio that evening before taking me home and putting me to bed. Yes, our night was spoiled. That was life. I made a mistake. We laughed, we continue to laugh, we learned, we continue to learn; we moved on. Although she hasn't planned any extravagant anniversary celebrations since that night...

Ignaz Semmelweis

His name is Ignaz Semmelweis. The place is Vienna, Austria. His story is well known among healthcare providers. In 1847, Dr. Ignaz Philipp Semmelweis worked in Vienna General Hospital's first obstetrical clinic. In this capacity, Semmelweis had the opportunity to observe the effectiveness of the obstetric service provided by the hospital. The services were split into two obstetrics units, one staffed by doctors in training, the other staffed by midwives in training. At the time, there were considerable risks associated with pregnancy and childbirth to both mother and baby. Puerperal fever, also known as childbed fever, was the most significant maternal killer. Known today as a serious form of septicemia, at the time the causes were unknown and many doctors assumed the condition was unpreventable. Yet, as Semmelweis saw between the two units at the hospital, the maternal mortality rate in the midwifery unit was two to three times lower than the rate in the doctor's unit. Clearly the midwives doing something that he and his fellow doctors were not, or not doing something that the doctors were—but what?

Semmelweis knew that doctors would sometimes move directly from autopsies in the morgue to attending childbirth without washing their hands in between. One of his own friends died from an infection after puncturing his skin with a knife during the postpartum examination of a patient who died of puerperal fever. Semmelweis believed that there was something, perhaps particles from the cadavers, which the doctors were transferring to the mothers (the germ theory we all take for granted today would not be developed until decades later by Louis Pasteur and others).

To test his theory, Semmelweis instituted a policy that required caregivers to wash their hands with a solution of chlorinated lime between autopsies and the examination of patients. Given our current understanding of the criticality of hand hygiene, discovering that doctors moved from autopsy to mothers in labor without washing their hands makes the skin crawl. Yet, Semmelweis met resistance from medical students and hospital staff. He was, however, somehow able to enforce compliance in his clinic and consequently saw maternal death rates drop from 18.27 percent to 1.27 percent in the doctors' division. In both March and August of 1848, there were no deaths in his maternity ward—a direct result of his hand-washing initiative.

While Semmelweis's work was seminal in understanding how one could die from a hospital-acquired infection, the problem persists today. According to a Center for Disease Control (CDC) study conducted in October 2002, hospital-acquired infections lead to approximately 274 deaths in the U.S. every day. That's 100,000 people a year who will die from an infection they caught within a hospital in the U.S. alone. Set against the other causes of death, hospital-acquired infection becomes the fifth-leading cause of death in the U.S. behind heart disease, cancer, stroke, and chronic lower respiratory disease. If classified among accidental causes of death, hospital-acquired infection leads to more deaths than automobile accidents, poisonings, falls, suffocations, and fire combined (excluding other medical mistakes).

The question is whether these deaths can really be classified as accidental? The CDC publishes guidelines for the prevention of healthcare-acquired infections, including guidelines for hand hygiene. These rules stem from Semmelweis's early discovery that infections could pass between humans. Proper compliance with hand hygiene rules was the centerpiece of Semmelweis's infection control model and it's the centerpiece of the CDC's recommendations. Ask any nurse the number one thing that healthcare professionals can do to prevent healthcare-acquired infection, and they will likely respond, "wash our hands."

Essentially, the instructions for any healthcare provider are to wash before seeing the patient, after seeing the patient, after touching inanimate objects, before eating, and after using a restroom. The hand-washing protocol allows for using either antibacterial gels or washing with traditional soap and water.

Seems rather simple, right? What might you then expect the compliance rate to be for these mandatory policies in every hospital? You might guess 99 percent compliance or higher. It only seems reasonable that compliance rates would be very, very high. Yet, the data for U.S. hospitals averages around a 60 percent rate of compliance. More than 150 years after Semmelweis's discovery, we are sitting at a compliance rate of 60 percent. For each ten times that require hand washing, there are four breaches of policy.

Nearly every hospital in the U.S. has a hand hygiene initiative with buttons, posters, and any creative idea they can come up with to raise compliance rates. Some hospitals have taken to putting a dye on staffs' hands that shows them under a black light the bacteria that they carry around the hospital and transfer to their patients. Some hospitals have taken to threats of employment action such as time off or termination for those who do not comply. After all, we're talking about 100,000 lives a year—the number one "accidental" killer in the U.S.

But, again, are these deaths really accidental? Can it be mere human error alone that is causing a 40 percent rate of non-compliance? Our research with nursing, pharmacy, and physician groups shows that the 40 percent non-compliance rate is not necessarily caused by mere human error, such as simply forgetting to comply.

We cannot, however, jump to the other end of the spectrum and believe that our nation's healthcare workers are recklessly endangering the lives of millions of patients, knowingly killing 100,000 of our loved ones along the way. The healthcare provider that consciously says, "Today I choose to put my patient in harm's way," is a very, very small minority of providers. Again, it's not the reason behind a 40 percent rate of non-compliance.

As outsiders, we might not understand how a collective group of people could be only 60 percent compliant with a rule tied to the loss of 100,000 lives per year. Yet, most managers within healthcare are looking for a magic bullet that will reduce the intractably high rates of non-compliance. What looks like an easily resolved problem is really quite complex. In life, we are inundated with rules, regulations, guidelines, and recommendations. Follow the food pyramid, drink 64 ounces of water a day, floss two times a day, brush your teeth three times a day, exercise three times per week, follow the speed limit, don't talk on a cell phone, put the kid in the back seat strapped in properly—it's overwhelming when you think about it.

I have only known a few people in my life that even give the impression of following all of the rules. The rest of us are just trying to get by, just trying to get through the day without having a catastrophic failure. We look at those never-ending requirements and recommendations, and we choose. Is it laziness? No. Is it an uncaring attitude for those around us? No. It is instead the recognition that we cannot do it all. Sometimes, it's the recognition that the rules are inconsistent and that to follow one requires violating another.

My favorite example of this is in the movie *Raising Arizona*. John Goodman plays a petty criminal engaged in robbing a "hayseed" bank out in the desert of Arizona. He bursts through the front doors and shouts to the unlucky bank patrons, "Alright you hayseeds, it's a stick up.

Everybody freeze. Everybody down on the ground." At this point, all of those hayseeds just stare at John Goodman and his partner in crime. Sort of that deer in the headlight look, until one of the "hayseeds" rightly asks, "Well, which is it, young feller? You want us to freeze or get down on the ground? Mean to say, if'n I freeze, I can't rightly drop. If'n I drop, I'm gonna be in motion. You see…" It's at this point that John Goodman's character loses it and yells at the old codger, "Shut up! You can just forget that part about freezing."

Life is indeed complex, and sometimes downright confusing. We have to pick what is important to us, with a large set of inputs helping us make our choices. In the real world, some of these inputs are not particularly noble. Will I get caught? Will I get punished? Will my friends or family look favorably upon my choices? Will compliance get in the way of other goals?

Before we get on our soapbox with the healthcare provider, let's consider our own choices. First, hand hygiene. We all know we should wash our hands after using the restroom; given the high propensity for clean running water in most restrooms, one might expect near 100 percent compliance. Yet, go in a public restroom and collect (covertly) some data. You may be hard pressed to find the 60 percent compliance rate we see across hospitals. And this is likely the only time during the hour we'll need to wash our hands, unlike the healthcare provider who may have fifty hand-washing occasions during a one-hour period. For disease prevention, we all know that we should be washing our hands when leaving the restroom. If you have the Y chromosome (being a male), you are already statistically more likely than your female peers to be non-compliant in the public restroom and in the hospital as a healthcare provider. If you are alone in the restroom, you are also statistically more likely to skip hand washing. Why? Because there is no one there to see you!

We can all intellectually agree that proper hand hygiene after using the restroom is a good thing. (That's fifteen seconds scrubbing with soap and water, by the way, not three seconds of streaming water.) So why is it we are so non-compliant? Too much to do to take an extra fifteen seconds out of our day except when others are watching? Or is it that we convince ourselves that our one little instance of non-compliance will not dramatically alter the landscape of communicable disease?

This is the zone of behavior we refer to as at-risk behavior. It is where we convince ourselves that we are operating in a safe place, but where others observing our behavior view the choice as unjustifiably risky. It is a matter of perspective with the observer, that other person, judging your behavior as unacceptably risky while the observed, you, believes that the choice is justifiable and safe. It's me yanking the vacuum cleaner electrical cord out of the socket from 10 feet away, with my wife, or even my kids, seeing the behavior as an electrical short waiting to happen. To me it's convenience; to them, it's risky and disrespectful to the vacuum cleaner cord.

Consider the task of following the speed limit. First, one

group, the highway safety engineers, decides that a road is to have a 45 mph speed limit. Now drivers take to the completed road considering the meaning of that posted 45 mph speed limit. To many, it appears like Captain Barbossa's reference to the pirate code in the movie *Pirates of the Caribbean*, more of a *guideline* than a rule. Drivers look at the width of the road, the weather conditions, visibility at intersections, presence of pedestrians along the side of the road, and importantly, the speed of other vehicles on the road. Oh, and they're probably also considering at what speed the police are likely to pull them over.

As drivers, we choose a speed we think is right; let's say 52 mph. The rule is 45, but we choose 52, following the speed of nearly everyone else on the road. We balance our desire to arrive safely at our destination with our desire to arrive there sooner. Are we saying that we don't really trust highway safety engineers to set the correct speed limit? No. We seemingly just view their speed limit sign as only one input into our decision.

It is important to distinguish us driving at 52 mph, knowingly 7 mph over the speed limit, from that fancy Corvette driving at 80 mph in a 45. We are both non-compliant, yet most of us believe the Corvette, zipping along at 80, is being reckless—whatever that label means (see next chapter). We'll agree that we knowingly violated the rule, but we defend that we were not reckless with other people's lives. We argue some form of social utility or benefit, that our conduct allowed us to get home a bit faster without appreciably increasing the risk of an accident, given we are in total (at least we believe) control of our car. We might also argue that to go slower than the rest of the traffic, by following the speed limit, would in itself be a risky decision. At-risk behaviors exist in many aspects of our lives. We might be a little loose with financial decisions or push office flirting a bit too far. For some professionals, such as healthcare providers or airline pilots, at-risk behaviors can be deadly. A pilot may choose not to use a checklist because he believes, after hundreds of successful flights, that he has memorized the steps in a pre-flight check. True, he has them memorized, and every time he mentally recalls the checklist he has a successful flight. Yet, his behavioral choice to perform the task by memory is more risky than the decision to pull out the checklist and follow it step-by-step. Perhaps the risk of omitting a critical step goes from one in 10,000 when following the steps line by line (because he could still skip a step), while the risk of skipping a step in recall by memory is one in 1,000.

We look in as outsiders, assess the risk, more qualitatively than quantitatively, and weigh that increased risk against the utility or benefit associated with the choice. What social utility or advantage does the pilot gain by doing the task by memory? What other task is the pilot able to do when he or she doesn't take the time to use the checklist? We look in as outsiders and judge the conduct of our fellow human beings. Perhaps we say, "Yes, not much value added. I'd skip the step, too." Or we observe and decide that the increased risk is not worth the reward. While our friend engaged in the behavior may see it differently, we label it "at-risk," a label that implies a difference of opinion on the trade between risk and reward.

Intellectually, we all know not to speed on the road, to wear our seat belt, be courteous to others, eat healthy, brush our teeth three times a day, drink lots of water, and exercise regularly. Intellectually, I knew that it was important to read the label on the Benadryl package. I did not choose to fall asleep on my date with my wife, that was a mistake. But I did choose not to read a medication label, that was an at-risk behavior. (And this from a guy who has built quantitative risk models of medication safety risk at hospitals across the country.) That said, knowing the risk intellectually is one thing, being able to practically apply that knowledge is yet another.

How does our current culture address at-risk behavior? Strangely, we promote or we whack depending upon the outcome it yields. Consider the case of speeding on the road—those seven additional miles per hour calculated to keep up with other traffic, that wiggle room where you believe you are still in a safe place. We encourage it. In fact, when we find ourselves behind a driver actually driving the speed limit in that left, high-speed lane on the freeway, how often do we get annoyed? Might we flash our lights, honk our horns, perhaps, flip the guy off? We expect the other drivers to engage in the at-risk behavior with us. That is, until there's an accident; then, we only need to know that the driver was speeding for us to stand in judgment of the same behavior we endorsed before it occurred.

For at-risk behavior it's a no harm, no foul world. We

encourage the behavior until harm occurs, then we whack the offender, in large part because he violated a policy or broke a law. We seemingly all want to be able to engage in the at-risk behavior for the benefit we gain from it, yet, when things go wrong, we want some basis for taking action. We want someone to blame, and it's the person who chose the at-risk behavior who makes an easy target.

205 Tilley

Two hundred and five miles per hour. No, it's not a Formula 1 racecar or the approach speed of a Boeing jet aircraft. It is instead Sam Tilley from Stillwater, Minnesota. He's known in the motorcycle community as 205 Tilley. His fame comes from his participation in the annual "Flood Run," a motorcycle rally from Lake St. Croix Beach to Hastings, a 220-mile drive down Highway 61 alongside the St. Croix and Mississippi Rivers. The run began as a group of volunteers providing sandbagging support during the flood of 1965. Now it's become an annual motorcycle rally.

In 2004, the then 20-year-old motorcycle enthusiast participated in the rally on his Honda RC51, a 999cc sport bike. What earned him his fifteen minutes of fame was the state patrol pilot who clocked his motorcycle traveling at 205 miles per hour. Sam Tilley became an instant folk hero in the motorcycle community—half hero, half villain. He had apparently set a record for the fastest speed clocked on an actual highway, a record that has been subject to debate since his motorcycle would (as dynamometer testing would later suggest) go no faster than 159 mph.

Tilley was charged with three offenses: speeding, driving without a motorcycle license, and reckless driving. Tilley pled guilty to two counts, speeding and driving without a license, and in return the prosecutors dropped the reckless driving charge. For 205 Tilley, it meant one year of probation and 200 hours of community service.

Imagine yourself out for a Saturday drive on Highway 61, your lovely spouse in the passenger seat beside you, talking about the grandchildren and enjoying the beautiful Mississippi vistas, clipping along in your convertible at 75 mph (10 miles over the 65 mph limit). Yes, you're knowingly violating the law by speeding, but it's such a beautiful drive and your shiny new convertible performs so smoothly and capably that you can't help but believe that 75 mph is a safe speed.

In your rearview mirror you see what appears like a low flying airplane coming up on you quickly. He flies by you at 205 mph. That's 130 mph faster than you! As he passes, you notice that the aircraft is actually a motorcycle, moving at extraordinary speed. Two hundred and five miles per hour of extraordinary speed! You cannot help but turn to your mate and sputter, "Did you see that? Can you believe that guy? He's so dangerous! He's so reckless! Where's a police officer when you need one? I hope he gets busted!"

The act of going 205 mph clearly crosses into the zone of reckless behavior. You might not have a definition, but you know it when you see it: reckless.

The Minnesota statute under which Sam Tilley was prosecuted reads as follows:

169.13 (a) RECKLESS DRIVING.

Any person who drives any vehicle in such a manner as to indicate either a willful or a wanton disregard for the safety of persons or property is guilty of reckless driving and such reckless driving is a misdemeanor.

We'd all agree that there comes a point where our wiggle room with regard to speed "guidelines" clearly crosses a line from being merely non-compliant with the law to being an individual who is knowingly or willfully putting others at risk. That person has crossed over to reckless behavior. There are many words both the law and society have used to describe it, from egregious to wanton, from gross negligence to willful blindness. The term we use is reckless.

Recklessness is different than the mere decision to speed. One is a mere violation of the rules; the other is, well, reckless. Consider Minnesota's guidance to drivers around the topic of speeding:

"The faster you drive, the less time you allow yourself to react to events on the road and around you. Traveling at faster speeds increases the likelihood of crashes. And when crashes occur at higher speeds, victims' injuries tend to be more serious and death is more likely to result. Minnesota law requires you to drive at a speed no faster than is reasonable under existing conditions. These include weather, traffic, and road conditions. Driving faster than the posted speed limit is illegal."

It's not the right thing to do, it's illegal. There you have it. However, if you get pulled over by a police officer for speeding in the state of Minnesota, or any state for that matter, there is only a very small chance you will receive a ticket for reckless driving, even though the state of Minnesota believes that speeding needlessly increases the risk of death. Speeding results in a fine (one could argue it's a small fine given Minnesota's statement that the risk of death increases as speed increases). Reckless driving, on the other hand, would get you a potential fine of $700 and up to ninety days in jail (based on published year 2000 penalties).

While we might like to think that breaking the law is breaking the law, we do differentiate between the reckless and the at-risk violation. We know that going 65 mph in a 55 mph zone is "wrong." Yet, as a society, we're willing to tacitly accept that, as drivers, we will regularly choose to go 65 mph in a 55 mph zone, perhaps because we believe, rightly or wrongly, that the risk does not appreciably change with this decision. In fact, if the only thing we valued was safety when driving, and we know that higher speeds correlate to a higher likelihood of death, why don't we universally set the speed limit at 40, 25, or even 10 mph? We are forced to decide what is acceptable risk when compared to the benefits. The highway engineers take the first stab at it. Then, we as drivers make our own choices.

Like the pirate code, speed limits seem to act more like guidelines. We individually choose what we believe to be a "safe" speed and, if we choose to go faster than the speed limit, we take our chances with a speeding ticket. When we get caught, we sheepishly pay the fine, take the driver's safety course to reduce the potential effects on our insurance rates, and then continue with our rather complex system for deciding future driving speeds.

Reckless behavior is that behavior where we as a group clearly believe that the risk outweighs the rewards. We see the risk as substantial and unjustifiable. We believe that anyone who chooses the behavior does so in full recognition of the risk as both substantial and unjustifiable. We condemn the behavior. Drunk driving, extremely excessive speed, riding in the back of an open pickup, text messaging while driving. We know them when we see them; we call them reckless.

In our work capacity, we are not likely to see much reckless behavior. A physician, a pilot, or a police officer is not likely to engage in much reckless behavior. When one of them does, it tends to become national news—the pilot who arrives for duty still drunk from the night before; the anesthesiologist who kills his young patient as a result of his own illicit drug use; the police officer who's a little quick with the trigger in the immigrant neighborhood.

There are three reasons for this. First, what makes a behavior reckless is that the risk is universally seen as outweighing the reward; it's substantial and unjustifiable, and it's ignored. This differs from at-risk behavior where we convince ourselves that the risk is worth taking, or we don't see the risk at all. The second reason is that reckless behavior usually results in a sanction of some sort—termination, probation, license revocation. It is at the threshold of reckless behavior, the conscious disregard of a substantial and unjustifiable risk, that we are called to action with the individual perpetrator.

The third reason we don't see a lot of reckless behavior in the workplace is that choosing recklessness requires some other goal that out-prioritizes the risk of harm the behavior might cause to others. In a work situation, there's just not much pay-off for reckless behavior in the same way there is in our off-work activities.

For example, there are few people who want to get behind the wheel of their car and drive drunk. But as court dockets clearly indicate, many are willing to drive drunk if it means they can have fun with friends at the pub across town. They have prioritized fun over the risk of causing harm to themselves or others by their decision to drive drunk. There is a benefit in their willingness to be reckless with themselves and others. For a pilot in the cockpit of an aircraft or a nurse at bedside, there will likely not be those other interests at play. Yes, you may find a nurse with a drug addiction or a pilot with affections for a flight attendant, who is willing to take unreasonable risks to meet his goals—but not many and not often. Human errors and at-risk behaviors are prevalent in the work world; reckless behavior is not.

In our discussion around recklessness, it's important to understand that the person who engages in reckless behavior still does not *intend* to cause harm. We reserve words like "purpose" to describe that type of intent. Murder is a crime of "intent," and there is some general agreement on what justice means in that context. Recklessness can be found in the intoxicated driver whose goal was to enjoy his evening at the pub. The choice to drive home intoxicated was not a choice to kill someone on the road; it was a choice to knowingly put others at risk (ignoring, for the moment, any arguments about the decision-making capacity of the intoxicated).

We all take risks in life. We all make choices, weighing one risk against another. Will I drive with the slightly flat tire? What is the risk, what is the reward? Will I let my child play on the park equipment? What is the risk, what is the reward? We do this analysis every day in every aspect of life. Recklessness is when we do the analysis, we see the risk as substantial and unjustifiable, yet we still choose to take the risk to put ourselves or others in harm's way. That said, we still, in our heart, hope or pray that no harm occurs. That's the general nature of reckless behavior.

Consider your children, or if you are not a parent, think about what it must have been like to be your parent. We see that children make mistakes. It's part of growing up. We see children make risky choices, but they believe that their actions are somehow justified under the circumstances. Perhaps it's an 8-year-old riding that bicycle a tad bit too close to the new family car, ripping off the side view mirror in the process. Or perhaps it's the kindergartner who, in a creative burst, uses the passenger side of the car as a canvas for the flower she etches with a rock. These are likely at-risk behaviors where the child (depending on her age) probably should have recognized the increased risk of harm—but didn't.

Then there are the reckless behaviors where parents must assess their children's actions and determine that they absolutely had to know the risk they were taking. You turn to your spouse and say, "Honey, do you think there's any way that child of yours could believe that setting off automobile safety flares in the woods was a reasonable thing to do?" In such a situation, parents make the judgment call, decide their child engaged in reckless behavior, and then take action.

So how does society deal with reckless behavior? Well, it's back to a modified version of no harm, no foul. We will generally condemn the reckless behavior, irrespective of any undesired outcome. That said, the severity bias still creeps in. Consider attitudes around college drinking. Many college students might ignore, if not praise, the drunk driver who got home without incident. It was success, not failure— regardless of the underlying reckless actions or the increased potential to cause harm. If the student got pulled over on the way home from the bar, his friends might be sad he got caught, but they would understand the relatively severe response—a night in jail, perhaps a loss of his license. But how will they respond if their friend hits another car, taking out a young family? Now, the classmate is facing more than a year in jail, his conduct judged a felony. Same behavior, same reckless tag, but it is the severity of harm that ultimately decides his fate.

You might rightly ask, "Why does it matter whether the drunk driver actually gets into an accident?" Why does the penalty not relate to the quality of the behavioral choice, rather than the luckiness or unluckiness of the drunk driver? Reckless is reckless, yet we seem to afford some grace to the lucky reckless person that is not afforded to the unlucky reckless person engaged in the same reckless behavior. Does this make any sense at all?

Console, Coach, or Punish?

Our adult version of Whack-a-Mole says this: look at the outcome, turn a blind eye to bad system design and risky behavioral choices until that mole, that undesirable outcome surfaces, then whack 'em. Severity of harm is the linchpin of accountability in our society today. Where does the differentiation of human error, at-risk, and reckless come into play? In the adult world, it often doesn't. Ask a group of healthcare practitioners what leads to disciplinary sanction in their hospital, and they will report that it's the severity of harm. You know—no harm, no foul.

Consider, if you will, an alternative to our outcome-based Whack-a-Mole approach. What should "justice" look like for the human error, the at-risk behavior, and the reckless behavior? Should the three behaviors be treated differently? Is Sam Tilley different than the father who left his child in the car on a hot day? Are the parents who inadvertently injure or kill 45 of their young children each year by forgetting them in the family car, any different than the millions of us who are a bit loose around our hand hygiene habits?

Remember, human error is the inadvertent action. At-risk behavior is, generally, the knowingly non-compliant place where there's a difference of interpretation around the behavior, where the observed believes they are still in a safe place but the observer judges otherwise. The reckless behavior is the choice to consciously disregard a substantial and unjustifiable risk. These are three different behaviors arising from three different causal mechanisms.

All three, however, may involve a breach of duty. Whether I inadvertently back over my neighbor's mailbox (an error), or I fail to turn my head when backing up (an at-risk behavior), or I choose simply to not even look in the rearview mirror (the reckless act), I still have run over my neighbor's mailbox.

If my neighbor were standing on her front doorstep watching as I destroy the mailbox, her emotional reaction might be different based upon what she observed in my behavior. Regardless, I would have breached the duty I owe my neighbor—the duty we all owe each other not to harm persons or property—and I would be responsible for remedying the harm. I could rebuild the mailbox or pay for its repair. Paying for the damage we cause or the mistakes we make, regardless of the reason, is the basis of the American approach to justice. This approach serves two purposes: paying for our damages acts as a deterrent to making the same mistake twice, and payment restores the damaged party to wholeness.

Now put yourself in the role of parent, teacher, or boss. You have a child, student, or an employee who is working for you. They make a mistake or a bad choice. How will you respond? Will you judge the human error, the at-risk behavior, and the reckless behavior differently? The answer is that you will; however, there will be other factors, such as the severity of the outcome, which will significantly impact your decision-making process.

What we know from the review of many social systems (workplace, sports, everyday life) is that the severity of the harm often dictates how severe the response will be. Had Sam Tilley run into a car, pulling out onto Highway 61, would he have received only probation and community service? The question is, perhaps, nonsensical in this instance; had Sam Tilley hit a car at 205 mph, he would not have been alive to punish. Regardless, the behavioral choice would have been the same and had he survived our hypothetical accident, he would have been dealt with much more severely.

Look at the front page of your favorite newspaper and you will see this trend: how bad was it, who is to blame? The greater the harm, the more eager we are to punish. We look at the last person in the causal chain and point an indignant finger at them. The pilot in the aircraft accident, the nurse or physician in the medical mistake—all are likely to have an accusative finger pointed at them. The question is whether this strategy gets us where we want to be?

Throughout this book, I make the argument that there are really only two inputs impacting our ability to avoid adverse events. The first is the design of the system in which we put ourselves, our children, our employee, or the person whose professional career we're tasked to oversee as a government regulator. The second input is the behavioral choices of the people within those systems. Choices. What we do not have such immediate control over are the human errors that we make, nor the adverse outcomes we produce, even when trying our best. Our control rests solely in the systems we design and in the behavioral choices we make within those systems.

Consider the classic literary work, *The Little Engine That Could*, by Watty Piper. I read the book as a child, then again as an adult in my quest for admission to law school. Not having the most stellar undergraduate grades in engineering school, I needed to have a great test score to get into law school. So I took a prep course in order to score better on the Law School Admissions Test (LSAT). The course met for weeks, multiple times a week. I wasn't cramming new knowledge into my head, but instead learning how to take tests, particularly the LSAT. We learned how questions were written and how to tackle solving the given problems. It was great stuff, and it made a difference.

At the front of the room where I took the course, the instructor had a copy of *The Little Engine That Could*. On the last day of the class he told us all to buy the book and read it the night before the test. I did just that. Here I was, 32 years old, reading a childhood book in preparation for the LSAT. It worked. I did very well on the test and got into law school.

So what is it that worked? In the book, if you will recall, the Little Engine is a bit underpowered. Her job is to move single cars around the train yard. The big engines carry the big loads over the mountain passes. In the story, the Little Engine is asked to help a big steam engine because he couldn't make it alone. As the Little Engine approaches the pass, she keeps saying to herself, "I think I can, I think I can, I think I can." And, as you probably know, she did just that. She conquered the mountain pass, willing herself, believing in herself.

No one can discount the effect of a six-year-old soccer player saying to herself, "I think I can, I think I can." Believing in one's self is surely important. That said, I do not want to be on the surgical table, with the neurosurgeon poking around my spine saying to himself, "I think I can, I think I can."

I don't believe that my success on the LSAT was because I willed myself to succeed; my system would have been unreliable had it relied solely on willing myself to not make errors. My success was a direct result of my system design (the decision to take the prep course), and my behavioral choices within that system (doing the homework). Reading the book was a good distraction to reduce pre-test stress, and it perhaps had some intangible effect on my psyche going into the test. The more important piece, however, is the work I did to prepare to take the test.

So what then do we do with the human error when it is a product of those two inputs, system design and behavioral choices? The answer, again, whether it is home life or work life, is to direct our attention away from the severity of the adverse event and the human error that caused it and toward the design of the system and behavioral choices of the humans in those systems. Toward the human error itself, the answer might simply be to console the person who made the mistake. No one wants to make mistakes. Children do not generally intend to spill their milk, you and I do not intend to drive through red lights, and our airline pilot does not intentionally pull onto the wrong runway. The origins of the error are the same; it's only the potential for harm that differs. Out of compassion—there, but for the grace of God, go I—we should simply console that human being for their human error regardless of the outcome.

This does not, of course, end the inquiry or end any hope of holding anyone accountable for the adverse event. Who was accountable for the system design? What choices did the erring individual make? The human error itself and the adverse event are outcomes. Rather than look to the outcome, we should look instead to the actions that led to the outcome. That's where accountability lies.

At an individual level, assuming we are looking at a person in a system not of his or her own design (generally, the situation in the workplace), we still have the at-risk and reckless behavior to consider. It could be that in creating an adverse event, or an unacceptable risk, that someone made some bad behavioral choices. Perhaps it was the choice to do the task by memory rather than following the written instructions. Rather than stand in judgment of the mistake, we would instead stand in judgment of the behavioral choice to do the task by memory. Suppose the same person, however, was relying on written instructions but just missed a step. What then? We're back to consoling—there but for the grace of God...

Consider this in the case of road accidents. A car runs a red light, hitting a minivan carrying a family. What do we judge? The outcome to the family, the error of running the red light, or the fact that the driver who ran the red light was intoxicated? From a system safety perspective, we should look at the intoxication of the driver. Emotionally we'll judge the outcome and look to the person who caused the accident, the driver who ran the red light. Setting our emotions aside, if we are to punish the driver, it must be for the decision to drive intoxicated, not on whether he took a life. It is his choice, his choice to drive drunk, for which society must hold him accountable. Regardless of the outcome, console the human error and punish the reckless behavior.

The most problematic of the three behaviors is the at-risk behavior. We all engage in them, whether on the road, at work, or in our personal relationships. We convince ourselves we are in a safe place even when outside observers and the data might say otherwise. The drunk driver was on the road with fellow drivers who themselves were likely speeding, talking on cell phones, adjusting iPods, or engaging in other risky behaviors. As drivers, we engage in at-risk behaviors *en masse*. Some of these risky behaviors are even against the rules, but as we've already seen, rules are not the only factors that influence our behavioral choices.

We should be cautious about believing punishment is a "just" response to at-risk behavior. After all, nearly all human beings would be receiving some form of punitive sanction for their non-compliance with life's myriad rules. Instead, it is here where we talk about "coaching" as the proper response. Coaching, in this context, is not a reference to punishment, but is, instead, a non-punitive, constructive dialogue. It is similar in form to the coaching that a high school football coach might engage in with a player. Or what we do with our children when we see them engaged in risky behavior. With my children, if I put them in time out or on restriction every time they did something risky, they'd never get out of their rooms. Instead, I coach them on the risk I see even if no adverse event occurs. (Sadly, even my own children try to use the no harm, no foul argument on their father: "But Dad, nothing happened.")

The question concerns risk. Do I see a colleague, friend, or family member engaging in a behavior that appears risky, where they do not see the risk they are taking? Or perhaps they see the risk, but mistakenly believe it to be justified? I should coach them on the risk I see, regardless of the actual outcome. Here's the model in simple form:

Console the human error.

Coach the at-risk behavior.

Punish the reckless behavior.

Independent of the outcome.

It's a path that we see innovative regulators and corporate managers beginning to take. It's known in high consequence industries, such as aviation and healthcare, as a "just culture." We teach our employees that we are all fallible human beings. We expect them to learn from their mistakes, to help us design the safest possible systems around them, and we expect employees to try to make the safest possible choices in those systems. It's about setting aside the severity of harm and the actual inadvertent errors, and looking instead to the quality of the systems we have designed and the quality of the choices made in those systems. Console the error, coach the at-risk behavior, punish the reckless. Then, get on with the task of building a better system: changing performance shaping factors that subtly alter the rate of human error; adding barriers to prevent some classes of error; adding recovery steps to catch errors downstream before they lead to harm; and incorporating redundancy to minimize the impact of a failing system—these are the efforts that are going to produce better outcomes whether we're counting E's or working in a highly complex system.

It's expecting more by changing the nature of our expectations. It's a model of justice that works. It's what we do on our best days as parents, when we've had enough sleep to shore up our wells of patience. On our worst days, as parents, managers, or government regulators, well, we're not even close. On those days, it's Whack-a-Mole.

PART THREE

THE DUTIES WE OWE

In Part Three we add a bit of complexity. To be justly held accountable, we must first know for what we are accountable. Duty precedes error. To make a mistake, there had to be a "right" thing to do in the first place. This part explores the duties we impose on each other, and how these duties shape our systems of learning and systems of accountability.

A Single Cheeseburger

A single cheeseburger with mayonnaise, onion, tomato. That's been my order for the last twenty-five years. When I stop in for lunch at my generally reliable fast food burger shop, I pay the cash, and they deliver the food (fries and drink included).

It can be called a duty to produce an outcome. That is, I pay and the fast food restaurant has a duty to deliver my order—correctly is my expectation. Errors and the results of errors take a particular path under this type of duty. Over a few years' span where I was too regularly eating at this establishment, I would often receive lettuce along with my mayonnaise, onion, and tomato. It's a fairly small breach of duty, but noticeable nonetheless. Perhaps it was the familiar "lettuce, onion, tomato" that was leading them astray. After all, who orders onions and tomato without also requesting lettuce?

We've all had the experience of receiving food that did not match what we ordered. There is no procedure for what follows, only a social norm; if you did not get what you ordered, you can walk back up to the counter and get the order fixed. Or in my case, you simply remove the lettuce. What you don't do is offer to help. As a systems engineer, I must admit I have been tempted to jump over the counter to help, perhaps out of curiosity more than anything else. What is it in your system that compels you to routinely add the lettuce when I am confident I did not order it?

Think about the notion of shared accountability, where two people, or groups of people, work together to produce a desired outcome. This is not one of those cases. I do not "team" with my restaurant to produce the desired food. The social norm, or expectation, is that the burger shop owns the result; I, as their customer, simply stand in judgment. I cannot jump across the counter and offer to help. If I tried, I would meet considerable resistance. The rules of everyday life prohibit the intervention. If I do not like the fact that I get lettuce added to my burger, I can find another restaurant. It's that simple.

There are environments—the flight deck of an aircraft, the operating room of a hospital—where the person making the mistake participates in a learning system: a group of people get together to understand what happened and work together to design interventions that reduce the likelihood of future mistakes. It may be that the employees of the burger joint would do the same, but it would be internal to the restaurant. My relationship with the restaurant is simply to tell them that they produced the wrong outcome; they put lettuce on my burger. It is not a relationship of partnership or collaboration, but one of customer and supplier.

As the customer of the restaurant, I can only see the

mistake (the inadvertent outcome). I cannot see the system design, nor can I see the behavioral choices of those who put the lettuce on my burger. Did the lettuce get stuck on the hanging chad of an onion slice? Is it a windy kitchen, causing lettuce to fly around the room and inadvertently land on my sandwich? Or did the cook simply override my order and decide on his own that if I wanted onions and tomato, then I was going to receive lettuce as well? As the customer, I have no idea of the actual cause of the mistake. It is not my business. My contract with the restaurant does not include participation in the quality improvement process, other than to inform them of the undesired result.

Think about the social contexts where the duty to produce an outcome comes into play. For the most part, anything we purchase fits in this duty. We buy something and the supplier produces the result; there is no shared accountability. The rules of the road also fit into this category. Think of the rule that prohibits driving while intoxicated. The state prescribes the outcome: no driving while intoxicated. The state is not the least bit interested in why you're driving under the influence or what sequence of life events led you to this outcome. There is no shared accountability here; the state only cares that you're driving intoxicated.

When it comes to our duty not to drive while intoxicated, we are in complete control of the system that would prevent this from happening. The easiest way, of course, is not to drink at all. Nice idea in concept—but not very practical or desirable for a good portion of the population (remember Prohibition?). Alternatively, you could live in the city, where you take public transportation home from your evening of frolic. No car, no driving drunk. Another option is to choose a designated driver.

There are many ways we can avoid driving while intoxicated, none of which will matter to the police officer who pulls you over. The police officer only wants to verify that you have met the blood alcohol threshold for driving under the influence. The same is true for being caught speeding—the police officer only wants to show that you were above the speed limit.

The ticket you receive, or in the case of drunk driving, the incarceration you might receive, is meant to be a deterrent. The deterrence effect is that you might redesign your system (sell your car, perhaps), or make a set of different behavioral choices (give up drinking or give up driving).

The choices are generally left up to the offender. The police officers and the courts do not care about *why* you got in this mess. It was your job to design a good system and to make reasonable choices within that system. For the police officer, there is no human error, at-risk, or reckless behavior in the typical traffic violation. There is simply the duty to produce an outcome.

This duty to produce an outcome carries over into the workplace and the home as well. We ask our teenagers to clean their bedrooms. We specify what it means for the bedroom to be clean: no clothes on the floor, no dirty dishes, no foodstuff. But we do not generally tell our teenager how to clean the room (if we were diligent, effective parents we began teaching them how when they were just toddlers). The system for cleaning their room is up to them; the duty only specifies the result. We as parents, to whom the duty is owed, look only to the results.

In the workplace, the code of conduct is typically the centerpiece for the duty to produce an outcome. Get to work on time, wear a badge, be properly attired, and so on. There are times when we tell our child, employee, or those we regulate simply to produce a specified result. How they get there is up to them.

Consider the task of showing up to work with your badge. From the employer's perspective, there are only two visible results: you show up with the badge or you do not. For you, however, there is a complex set of interactions, systems and behaviors working together to produce this result. There is that key hook just inside the door where you enter the kitchen. Or perhaps there is that corner of your dresser, where you dump all the things from your pockets at the end of the day. The hook, the strategic location on the dresser—these are system elements. These are a part of your system design so that you show up to work each day with your badge.

Your behavioral choices are the next part of the equation. You're exhausted, so you don't use the hook inside the door to hang your keys and badge but instead leave the keys and badge on your desk in the study. Or perhaps you are one of those individuals who leaves their badge in their car, assuring through good system design that the badge is going back to work with you the next day. Yet, today, you simply forget to take the badge off, leaving it instead in the bathroom.

When your boss asks you the next morning where your badge is, you recall your system design, your good and bad behavioral choices, and your inadvertent mistakes. You are the owner of the system, and you controlled the behavioral choices in that system. You had the control. You owned the outcome. Your employer, on the other hand, could only stand in judgment of the result. He was the customer; you were the supplier. There is no human error, at-risk, or reckless distinction in the eyes of your boss, no shared accountability. Whether it was a mistake, an at-risk behavior, or reckless behavior is unimportant to your boss—you are simply not wearing your badge. There is no shared accountability here—only the requirement that you produce an outcome and show up to work with your badge properly pinned to your outerwear.

Would the typical employee be fired for showing up without a badge? No. Would the typical employee be fired if he or she never showed up with their badge? Possibly. Working in an office environment, our employer might be happy with a 90 or 95 percent rate of success.

If you work for an airline and your badge provides you access to the ramp area of the airport, your employer might only tolerate a few undesired outcomes. The business impact of showing up at the airport without your badge might prohibit you from performing your job at all, as access to the ramp would be prohibited by airport security. No badge, no work. Go home.

We design systems to produce results—but remember, our system design will never be perfect. Consider the task of getting to work on time. Your employer might say that you are allowed no more than three tardy days (not exceeding one hour) in every quarter. This provides you some clues to designing your system. Natural disasters, bridge collapses— these rare occurrences are likely not going to be held against you. But you'll still have to design your system to get you to work on time 95 percent of the time.

If you choose to live within walking distance of your job, getting to work on time should pose little problem. If your work involves a congested commute into the city and you are contemplating living in the less crowded suburbs forty-five minutes away, you are putting yourself at risk. Your system design (when you leave the house in the morning) would have to accommodate the variations in freeway congestion. You would assess the availability of alternative routes when the freeway is closed due to an accident or an overturned truck carrying hazardous waste. You would assess the reliability of your car. You would assess the reliability of your system of alarm clocks. If you were smart you would give careful consideration to the design of your system, knowing that you are a fallible human being and that some of the factors leading to delay might be out of your control.

It's called the duty to produce an outcome. The customer sets the expectation. The supplier designs the system and makes the right behavioral choices to meet the expectation. It is fair. It is just. The person who owns the system owns the result. If we as customers don't like the result or the error rate, we use our power to choose another supplier. That's the general model and unlike Whack-a-Mole, it's both effective and efficient.

When does our response to a failure of the duty to produce an outcome lead to our adult version of Whack-a-Mole? When we couple the duty to produce an outcome with the expectation of perfection. It's when we yell at our barista for giving us our latte with low fat instead of whole milk or our mocha with whipped cream when we clearly stipulated none. Mistakes happen; take the latte or the mocha back to the counter and the barista will remake it. If the rate exceeds your tolerance for error, you might rightly ask to speak to the manager. "Respectfully, sir," you might say, "I've been here three times this week. Each and every time I get low fat instead of whole milk."

The coffee shop manager has a duty to produce an outcome. He must design a good system around his employees and he must manage his employees' behaviors within that system. In response to your dissatisfaction with his shop's error rate, he'll be wise to consider what in his system design or his staff's behavioral choices might be leading to this repetitive error. Perhaps he color codes the containers holding the milk or keeps whole milk in one refrigerator and skim in another. Whatever his system improvement, expecting perfection out of our barista or the coffee shop manager will only lead to Whack-a-Mole. There is no system design that can ensure we'll get whole milk instead of skim in our latte 100 percent of the time.

100,000 Pages

May 25, 1979, O'Hare International Airport, Chicago, Illinois. Flight 191, an American Airlines DC-10 headed for Los Angeles, was cleared for takeoff at 2:59 p.m. Three minutes later, Flight 191 started down runway 32R. Just before the nose lifted off the ground the No. 1 engine and pylon came off the aircraft, rolled over the top of the wing, and fell to the ground. Despite losing one of its three engines, the plane lifted off about 6,000 feet down the runway, climbed out in a wings-level attitude, reaching an altitude of about 300 feet. Soon the aircraft began to turn and roll to the left, the nose pitched down, and the aircraft began a rapid descent. It crashed in an open field and trailer park over a mile northwest of the departure end of the runway.

The aircraft was destroyed on impact, instantly killing all 271 passengers and the flight crew; two more on the ground also lost their lives. Before the plane crashes of September 11, Flight 191 was the deadliest air accident in U.S. history.

The National Transportation Safety Board (NTSB) concluded that the aircraft rolled because the left wing slats (that provide lift) retracted, causing the lift to be greatly reduced on the left wing compared to the right wing. The reasons for the un-commanded retraction of the left wing slats were traced back to the installation of the left wing mounted engine nearly two months before the accident.

The maintenance manual for a modern jet airliner might be 60,000 to 100,000 pages long. Including component manuals for the parts on the aircraft, there can be millions of pages in maintenance manuals instructing technicians how to perform maintenance and repair on a modern jetliner. These manuals dictate how the work is to be performed. If an aircraft presents a problem, the technician has a fault isolation manual to help diagnose the cause. Once the technician determines the cause, the technician has a removal and installation procedure for how to remove the bad part and install the new one.

The Federal Aviation Administration (FAA) is serious about technicians following the rules. Federal Aviation Regulation 43.13, applicable to all aircraft maintenance technicians, reads in part as follows:

(a) Each person performing maintenance [...] shall use the methods, techniques, and practices prescribed in the current manufacturer's maintenance manual...

For airplane maintenance, the manufacturer generally determines how the work is to be performed. The airline technician is expected to follow the rules. This is the duty to follow a procedural rule. If the tire is flat, the manual dictates how to change the tire. If the engine is not working, the manual describes, in exact detail, how to change the engine.

In the case of Flight 191, the plane's left engine was changed 55 days before the catastrophic loss of the aircraft. In their investigation, the NTSB found that American Airlines maintenance technicians had developed an alternative means for removing the engine, based in part on perceived time constraints at the maintenance facility. Tragically, this alternate method physically stressed the pylon mounts on the wing, inadvertently fracturing the attachment bolts. As the aircraft rolled down the runway, the forces of engine thrust and the weight of the engine itself caused the engine to separate from the aircraft. The result was the nation's worst single aviation accident, traceable to a simple failure to follow procedural rules.

There are times in life, and particularly in high-risk or high-consequence industries, where the system designers expend enormous resources to build an optimal procedure. If left to the wisdom of each individual performing safety critical tasks, the risk is too great that one or more individuals might design an inefficient or even hazardous procedure.

Aviation, as an industry, is extremely procedurally rooted. Pilots are told how to fly the aircraft. Technicians are told how to maintain it. The stakes are just too high to leave the procedures to individual choice. Engineers have time and resources to work out procedures, to anticipate possible mistakes, and to work to mitigate their likelihood or impact before they occur. One minor alteration to the procedure, well intended or not, might mean the difference between profitability and loss. One slight alteration to the procedure might mean the difference between success and catastrophic failure.

Nearly every employer imposes the duty to follow a procedural rule on its employees. Many of us work in environments where lessons learned over many years have worked their way into the protocols of how the work is to be performed. For an employee, these procedures impose the duty to follow a procedural rule. The employee follows the procedure; the business organization owns the outcome. In complex environments it will be many employees working together, all doing their part to help the system meet its goals.

Under the duty to follow a procedural rule, we create a system of shared accountability. If we are the system designers, we are accountable for the outcome; the employee within the system is accountable for compliance. When things go bad, we learn together. We learn why the systems did not work, or we learn why the procedure was not followed. It is here that we attempt to understand, in relevant terms, why the breach has occurred. Did our employee inadvertently make a mistake in attempting to follow the procedure? Did our employee knowingly deviate, but under the belief they were in a good, safe place? Did our employee deviate from procedure because there was some other legitimate, compelling interest to be satisfied?

It is in the duty to follow a procedural rule, where

console, coach, and punish, applied to the human error, at-risk behavior, and reckless behavior is applicable. It is here we must create an open learning culture between those who create the procedures and those whose job it is to follow them.

Honey, Will You Wash the Dishes?

Washing the dishes. It's a relatively simple task, whether by hand or using the dishwasher. The dialogue goes something like this:

Honey, will you wash the dishes tonight?
Yes, dear.

A lot is packed in these two short statements. The first, through the eyes of a lawyer, is the offer. The second is the acceptance. Offer and acceptance. All that remains is consideration—the three elements of a contract. Now, in consumer worlds, the consideration is legal speak for the benefit or payment the doer would receive. Outside of the confines of the marital relationship (where keeping your mate happy trumps all other considerations), the rest of the dialogue might look as follows:

Son, will you wash the dishes tonight?
Two dollars?
Agreed.

This might be the scenario of a dad asking one of his children to take on the duty he has just accepted from his wife. Wife asks husband to do dishes, husband pays off child as the subcontractor. Offer, acceptance, and consideration. The subcontract is in place.

What's missing in this scenario is the nature of the duty; that is, what is really required of the person who accepts the duty to wash the dishes? We live with literally millions of little duties such as this. We're not talking about installing an engine on the wing of an aircraft or performing neurosurgery—just doing household chores, daily life stuff. Sometimes the duty is to produce an outcome—to be at an appointment on time. Other times, the duty is to follow a procedural rule in helping someone else produce a desired result. Sometimes, it's not so clear which duty it is, which brings us back to washing the dishes.

What is my wife really saying when she asks, "Honey, will you wash the dishes tonight?" To my mind, it would seem that inherent in the request lies the duty to produce an outcome of clean dishes, glassware, and utensils.

What happens in my house is as follows: I load the dishwasher, using all of my engineering skills to ensure that each plate, fork, or glass gets the best possible opportunity to get clean. I load the glasses and cups so that they are least likely to tip over and fill with soapy water. I load silverware to optimize the goal of clean utensils balanced against the threat that someone will be poked while removing the utensils (particularly knives). Many people (my wife included) apparently view dishwasher loading as an art, a puzzle requiring precision for all the pieces to properly fit together; for me it's simply about engineering design and meeting the goal of clean dishes.

So the dishwasher is loaded and washing away. I am on my way to the target outcome, working under the duty to produce an outcome: clean dishes. Then enters my wife. She strolls by the dishwasher, notices that it is still in the wash cycle, and stops. Without hesitation she opens the door. She pulls out the top rack, tactically loaded with glasses and long utensils. She watches, she contemplates, and she makes her move. She starts re-arranging the dishes.

It is deflating when you're working under the duty to produce an outcome, an outcome that you firmly believe is within your grasp, and the customer (to whom the duty is owed) jumps into your process and starts telling you how to do the job. It's the reason I don't jump over the counter at my local fast food burger joint to ensure I don't get a piece of soggy lettuce with my onions and tomato. It's socially unacceptable.

There is no Federal Dishwashing Administration telling me that I have to follow the manufacturer's instructions. While there is indeed an owner's manual providing written manufacturer instructions for loading the dishwasher, I'm both a guy and an engineer; we're not that apt to follow instructions on household appliances. We don't need them. In my professional life as an engineer, I've had to follow procedural instructions telling me how to do this, how to do that. All I'm asking for is a little latitude in washing my own dishes. For me, loading the dishwasher is an act of creativity—I get to decide how to do the job so long as I achieve the desired outcome. My wife has only asked that I wash the dishes, and that is what I am doing. My wife can stand in judgment of whether the dishes arrive in the cabinets at the proper level of cleanliness—but it's my job to determine how I get to that result.

If you talked to two of my younger children, those generally assigned to load the dishwasher, they'd tell a different story. They understand it is not a system of their design. In our house, Mom is the one who designed the dishwasher loading procedure (still unwritten at this point and seemingly, a moving target depending on which dishes are actually dirty), and the kids are tasked with working within the system of her design.

To my children, the duties around loading the dishwasher are procedural. Mom designed the system, the kids (and myself included) simply act as cogs in her grand dishwasher-loading scheme. This doesn't faze my children; they understand the duty and they simply try to load the dishwasher, following her loading rules as quickly as possible so they can get out the door and play.

But it bothers me; I just don't understand the duty. Is it a duty to simply produce an outcome of clean dishes? Or is it the duty to follow a procedural rule and load the dishwasher as my wife prescribes?

If I have the latitude to design the system as I wish, I am accountable for the result. The general rule is this: he who designs the system owns the result. If I said to my wife, "Poo-hah with that procedure! I'll do this my own way," I had better produce a clean set of dishes. I have chosen to own the system; therefore, I have chosen to own the result. There is no shared accountability here, just dishes that are clean or dirty, an outcome that I own personally.

In contrast, if I agreed to be a cog in my wife's system, to follow her procedure, I would then be accountable for compliance. Under this duty, I would not be warranting the result. Rather, I would simply try to be compliant and let the chips fall where they may. My wife, as owner of the dishwasher loading system, owns the result. I am merely the obedient husband, accountable only for my compliance or lack thereof. In this situation there is shared accountability; my wife owns the system and I own my behavioral choices within that system. To comply or not to comply, that is the question.

So what happens if the dishes come out dirty? If I've designed the system, I own the result. It is up to me to determine why the system failed. It is up to me to make changes to reduce the likelihood of further dishwashing errors. (If I've asked others to participate, such as my children, I would look to their compliance within my system of procedures and controls.) I would consider not only my dishwasher loading strategy, but also my behavioral choices within my system: were they at-risk, reckless, or merely human error? Perhaps I should have rinsed that plate with the now baked-on spaghetti sauce. Same for the fork with egg yolk stuck between the prongs. And that plastic bowl with the melted rim? Perhaps it was best to keep it out of the dishwasher altogether.

In the case of my wife designing the system, the inquiry would look a bit different. My wife might ask, "Honey, did you rinse that spaghetti plate before you put it in the dishwasher?" At this point, she's trying to understand where her system failed. I might respond, "Yes, I took it into the shower with me and scrubbed it for hours before putting it into the dishwasher." My willingness to follow my wife's dishwashing procedure, my willingness to participate in the learning process when things do not go as planned—that is where my accountability lies. My wife, the system owner, is responsible for the overall performance of the system, and I, as the obedient husband, am accountable for my decisions within the system of her making.

We make system design choices in one of these two ways. We either take control and ask others to comply, or we delegate an outcome and leave the system design to others. Think about this in the very simple and straightforward area of giving directions. Half of us prefer to be in control, asking only for the address so that we can determine our own way to the dinner party. Others prefer to get specific instructions; turn left here, turn right there. In many areas of our lives, it's often just a matter of preference. In some areas, particularly in high-risk industries, it's critical that personal preference not rule the day.

In high risk endeavors, such as flying a commercial airliner, working within a surgical unit, controlling the switching station for two commuter trains, or monitoring a nuclear power station, recognizing which duty you're operating under is critical to the outcome. Just ask those who lost loved ones in the American Airlines DC-10 accident over Chicago. This accident demonstrated clearly when a well-designed system of procedural controls will do better than merely asking employees to find their own path to the safe outcome.

Doing the Right Thing

Lawyers say it stems from the natural law. Doctors see it tied to the Hippocratic Oath. We learn it early from our parents. It's a rule seemingly embedded in our DNA, even though we too often fail to follow it.

First, do no harm.

It's the third duty, always taking precedence over the duty to produce an outcome and the duty to follow procedural rules. The first two duties are prescriptive, specifying outcomes and specifying "how to" procedures. The third, the highest duty, sits firmly atop the other two.

Many of us learned about the sinking of the *Titanic* in school. The *Titanic* was the unsinkable ship on its maiden voyage across the North Atlantic that struck an iceberg at 11:40 in the evening (ship's time) on April 14, 1912. It sank about two and a half hours later, killing 1,517 of its 2,200 passengers. Today the *Titanic* rests 12,500 feet deep at the bottom of the North Atlantic.

There were many contributors to the accident. Some argue that the ship was at excessive speed (22 knots) when it hit the iceberg. Some accounts suggest that J. Bruce Ismay, an executive with White Star Line who was on the maiden voyage, pressured the captain to go fast to make landfall ahead of schedule even though they were traveling in an area of known icebergs.

Coupled with the excessive speed was the reduced ability to see and avoid any upcoming icebergs. Up front on the ship is a crow's nest, a lookout point for crew to detect hazards ahead that is normally provisioned with binoculars. In the case of the *Titanic*, the binoculars were inaccessible; the key to the locker that held the binoculars had been accidentally left behind with a former crewmember. As a result, the crow's nest watch crew didn't see the iceberg until it was within 500 yards, not enough distance to prevent the collision.

Others look to the design of the ship that allowed six watertight compartments to flood, in part because of the angle that the ship hit the iceberg. There is some argument that had the ship steered into the iceberg, the damage to the ship might have been less.

Then there were the lifeboats. The law at the time required ships in excess of 10,000 tons to have sixteen lifeboats, enough available seats for 962 occupants. Unfortunately, there were 2,200 passengers and crew on board the *Titanic*, with capacity for more than 3,500. The White Star Line actually went beyond the regulation, adding four collapsible lifeboats, bringing lifeboat capacity to 1,178. Clearly not enough, though, for those on board. Compounding the problem on that bitter cold evening was that many of the lifeboats left the *Titanic* half empty. These boats did not go back for more passengers, perhaps fearing being sucked under by the sinking ship or being mobbed by stranded passengers.

Needless to say, this accident was not an "act of God." No earthquake, no lightning strike, no hurricane. Yes, there was an iceberg in the path, but that was a known hazard in that part of the North Atlantic. So who or what do we look to in this event? Was this human error? Or something more than a mistake?

The White Star Line was the operator of the *Titanic*. The British Board of Trade was the principal regulator. The regulator laid out rules for the design of the ship and the number of lifeboats on board. The White Star Line contracted with the passengers for safe passage across the Atlantic.

Safe passage was the outcome that every passenger expected. A fun filled trip across the Atlantic on the largest, most luxurious passenger ship afloat. In the case of the *Titanic*, the White Star Line clearly had a duty to produce an outcome; there was very little shared accountability here: passengers enjoy the ride, and the White Star Line ensures their safe passage across the Atlantic.

There were, perhaps, predictable errors and at-risk behaviors. Missing a piece of equipment, such as binoculars, was the result of mere human fallibility. The lifeboat issue, on the other hand, seems more than mere human error. It seems impossible to miscount—2,200 passengers, capacity for 3,547, yet lifeboats for only 1,178. Yet in this instance, White Star Line had met and actually exceeded the regulation by four lifeboats.

With hindsight it's clear the ship could have used more lifeboats. One rationale for the insufficient number of lifeboats is that they were intended only to ferry passengers between the ship in trouble and a rescue ship—provisioning lifeboats for all 2,200 passengers and crew seemed beyond the needs of any anticipated risks.

With the benefit of hindsight, it seems reasonable to require one lifeboat seat for every passenger and every crewmember. Most of us are not maritime safety experts. Few of us know the constraints that drove the design of ocean liners 100 years ago. We are all novices, yet we see in this tragedy a significant breach. If to err is human, and if an accident at sea is a predictable event, then it seems reasonable that White Star Line owed its passengers a means of emergency flotation.

We make this judgment as novices, not as ship safety experts. We make this judgment not based on what the regulations required, but against our life experience, our perceptions of risk, our understanding of risk versus rewards. Some risks in life are worth taking. Was skimping on lifeboats a risk worth taking? Most of us would say it was not. The White Star Line had breached its duty in the natural law by unjustifiably putting others in harm's way.

This natural law duty is not limited to the prevention of harm. It extends to the creation of risk. The duty to avoid causing unjustifiable risk, perhaps that's the better description. Imagine driving with a friend on the interstate, not much traffic around you, a few cars behind, and a few cars ahead. From a distance, you see a gray mirage up ahead. As you approach, you both recognize it as a fog bank that has rolled across the freeway. Your friend maintains his speed of 65 mph, shooting through the fog bank. You are inside the fog bank for probably ten seconds, in visibility of less than twenty feet.

As you clear the fog bank, your friend yells out, "Yahoo! We did it!" You look at your friend with round eyes, pupils dilated, astonished that he would not slow down as he traversed the fog bank. You challenge your friend, who responds, "What? I was doing the speed limit."

He's right—he was doing 65 mph, exactly what the regulations required. Yet, was the speed limit intended to rule the road when in a fog bank? Our assessment under these circumstances would not be rule-based. Whether our friend followed the rule or chose to violate it would be irrelevant. Instead our assessment would be risk-based. We would look to the risks taken: a car driving at 65 mph into a fog bank. Legality is not the issue at hand. We would instead look to the quality of the behavioral choice your friend made. Did he choose to put you at unjustifiable risk? Had the whole sequence of events been inadvertent, you and your friend would probably breathe a sigh of relief. However, because in this scenario your friend seemed to relish the experience, you would probably have some growing degree of disappointment or anger at your friend.

It's not a duty to produce an outcome or a duty to follow a procedural rule. This duty does not come from another human being's explicit instructions. Rather, it's out there in the ether, an element of most religions, a part of society's fabric. It's what we owe one another—the duty to not put others at an unjustifiable risk of harm.

No One to Help

Her name is Kitty Genovese. The story of her death is now more than forty-five years old. Catherine Susan Genovese was a 28-year-old New Yorker living and working in Queens as the manager of a sports bar. On the evening of March 13, 1964, she closed the bar, arrived home around 3:20 a.m. and parked about 100 feet from the entrance to her apartment. Winston Moseley, a business machine operator, had followed Genovese and was parked in a nearby railroad station. He caught up with Genovese after she got out of her car and proceeded to stab her in the back several times. Amid her screams, a neighbor reportedly yelled, "Leave that girl alone." Moseley fled, but soon returned to find the woman barely alive, lying in a hallway at the back of her apartment building. He stabbed Genovese repeatedly before sexually assaulting her. The attacks spanned approximately thirty minutes.

Kitty Genovese's murder is well-known to many even four decades later, in part because of a *New York Times* article written two weeks after her death by reporter Martin Gansberg. The headline read:

"Thirty-Eight Who Saw Murder Didn't Call the Police"

Gansberg's article generated considerable national outrage because (at least as told by Gansberg), thirty-eight bystanders were apparently unwilling to do anything—even something as anonymous as calling the police—to help Genovese in this vicious attack. Was it a callous disregard for the welfare of an unknown person? Did every witness assume that surely someone else had already called the police and they must be on their way? The outrage was so great, in fact, that the bystanders' behavior has become known as the "bystander effect" or the "Genovese Syndrome."

In the last chapter, we discussed the duty to avoid causing unjustifiable risk of harm. This was the third duty in the triangle, the duty that takes precedence over the duty to produce an outcome or the duty to follow a procedural rule. It's the duty that requires that we not be an agent of unreasonable risk to the 6 billion people who share the planet with us, to the other animals, or to the environment.

The duty to save is very different from the duty not to harm. In this duty, we represent a potential opportunity to save. In the case of Genovese, did anyone owe the duty to call the police? How fast were they required to call? Did those who heard her screams have a duty to give immediate aide? Should they have run into the street, putting themselves in harm's way to take on Moseley?

In hindsight, it is perhaps easy to take the high road, especially given the nature of Genovese's brutal attack and the number of people who stood by doing nothing. We are all perhaps convinced that had we been in that place at that time that we would have called, that we would have done something to save her. How could we not? It's a moral obligation.

Imagine another scenario. A dark, relatively deserted stretch of freeway. You see a woman standing by her car, stalled on the side of the road. Do you stop to render aid to preclude the possibility that she might be assaulted by someone else who stops? Do we think about our own safety and the safety of the three sleeping children in our own back seat? What if the woman is not really stalled? What if you had just heard a radio report of a rash of highway robberies under similar circumstances on this same freeway but several hundred miles away? What if this is just an elaborate set up for a robbery—or worse? We weigh the risks, we weigh the rewards, we choose (sometimes in split seconds) to take or not take action based on all of these considerations.

The duty to save is socially determined. There are some professions where the duty to save is just part of the job— firefighter, police officer, emergency room doctor, lifeguard. The duty to save is actually part of these professionals' job descriptions. There are other jobs where we might impose the duty to save: We might expect a daycare provider to do her best to put herself between a crazed intruder and her young charges. We'd likely expect a bus driver to keep jumping into the river to rescue his riders after the bridge collapse or a school crossing guard to do his best to pull a child from oncoming traffic. Even for parents, there's a clear social expectation that we run back into the burning house to rescue our own children.

To have a breach occur, however, the duty must first be present. For us to judge those who did not act when faced with Genovese's attack and subsequent death, we must first have imposed a duty upon them to act. If it is our belief that the bystanders breached their duty by observing and allowing the assault to continue, we judge them harshly. After all, none of her neighbors called the police, only one apparently yelled to the assailant to scare him off, no one walked into the fray risking physical harm to themselves to protect Genovese as the attack continued for more than thirty minutes. We cannot be angry with the bystanders unless we first believe they had a duty to act. They were clearly not the agent of harm; that was Moseley. Yet, they did have the opportunity to help prevent Genovese's death. They had the opportunity to possibly save her life. And, as many judged at the time, they had a duty to act.

Christopher Sercye

His name is Christopher Sercye, a 15-year-old living in Chicago, Illinois. On May 16, 1998, Sercye was shot by gang members while playing basketball near Ravenswood Hospital. One of the gunshots perforated his aorta. His friends dragged him to within 35 feet of the entrance to the emergency department. One companion ran into the emergency department, telling two police officers that his friend had been shot and lay bleeding on the sidewalk.

The police officers immediately told the ER staff. The staff, however, refused to give aide to Sercye. It was hospital policy that employees could not leave the ER. The rationale seemed to be that staff should take care of patients inside the ER, rather than touring the countryside looking for someone who might need help. Whatever the rationale, it was policy, and the ER staff were not about to breach their obligation to the rule. For fifteen minutes, Sercye lay bleeding at the bottom of the emergency room ramp, while ER staff followed their procedural rule. An ambulance was called to bring Sercye the 35 feet into the ER. Out of desperation, one of the police officers grabbed a wheel chair, put Sercye in the chair, and wheeled him through the ER doors. By that time, Sercye was still alive but the perforated aorta was taking its toll; he was pronounced dead forty-five minutes later.

Like the story of the Genovese assault, Sercye's death sparked a brief moment of national indignation. President Bill Clinton was so outraged that he threatened to remove Ravenswood Hospital from the list of hospitals eligible to receive Medicare payments if it did not change its policy.

Who killed Christopher Sercye? Three teenage gang members were charged in his death. They were the "evil hand," the direct cause. Yet, that was not the end of the story. Given the gunshot wounds, the perforated aorta, the internal bleeding—who was now responsible for saving Sercye's life? What duty would we impose upon his two companions? What duty would we impose upon the two police officers? The ER staff? The hospital administrators?

There were 5.9 billion people in the world in 1998. We

all had the duty not to shoot Christopher Sercye. It is part of the natural law to do no harm, to create no unjustifiable risk. None of us would argue that we should be allowed to hurt one another for no reason. There need not be a statute or a provision in a policy manual to tell us this. We just know it. Yet in the wake of Sercye's shooting, there was uncertainty about the duty to save. What duty did the ER staff owe the hospital? Following hospital policy surely would be one. What duty did the ER staff owe Christopher Sercye? Did they have an over-riding duty to save, a duty that would take precedence over the duty to follow the hospital's procedural rule?

We all have clear vision in hindsight. Yes, we now can see clearly the moral imperative to act. But being in the rush of the event would have been much different. We would all like to think we would have acted to save Sercye's life, just as we'd all like to think we would have done something to save Kitty Genovese or for the *Titanic* passengers begging us to return in our half-empty lifeboats. In hindsight, we're all good Samaritans, we all do the right thing.

In the case of Sercye, President Clinton imposed a duty to save—at least in the vicinity of hospitals. Today, the Emergency Medical Treatment and Active Labor Act (EMTALA) law requires that emergency rooms must respond to any presentation on the hospital campus. The law states that the campus is defined as any area within 250 yards of the main buildings. Public outrage to Sercye's death led to a new duty for hospitals. It's the duty to save.

Making Things Better

There's a road near my house that I take every morning on my way to work. It's the road that runs parallel to the freeway; its three lanes of traffic provide access to the businesses that line the freeway. At one point, the access road runs under an overpass, and in order for the drivers on the overpass to enter the freeway, they must first merge onto the access road and then they must shift across three lanes of traffic to merge onto the freeway filled with drivers making their daily commute into Dallas. As the name implies, the freeway provides (in theory) a commute unhampered by stops. In contrast, the access road has stoplights every mile that cause traffic to flow at a much slower pace than on the freeway, assuming the freeway is not backed up by an accident or normal rush hour congestion.

When I travel under this particular overpass, I am greeted most days with an unavoidable problem: a slew of cars trying to cross three lanes of traffic in passionate pursuit of the freeway entrance. If they are unsuccessful in merging, they are stuck on the access road and face a congested stoplight in a half-mile—a light that is notorious for needlessly torturing drivers with short spans of green lights. Drivers are clearly motivated to avoid this situation, to successfully enter the freeway, and begin the laborious, twenty-mile ride to downtown Dallas.

The commuters, so anxious to park their cars on the freeway, have only about 200 yards to transition across those three lanes of access road. They have to manage this with oncoming traffic (myself included) coming from the north at 50 mph, while they simultaneously accelerate to match freeway traffic. I can only hope they are looking over their left shoulders at least twice to be sure that crossing all those lanes is safe.

It is arguably a very poor design. A procedurally compliant driver, or perhaps a less risk-prone driver, would live with the fact that it is nearly impossible to cross three lanes of traffic in a 200-yard stretch, fighting on-coming traffic for lane space. The safe path is to simply live with the upcoming stoplight and merge onto the freeway another mile down the road where it is considerably safer.

But we're talking about the morning commute—and no self-respecting Texan is going to give up without a fight. So, the first driver in the chain of cars comes off the overpass, looks back over his left shoulder, perhaps checks the rear view mirror, sees a clear path, and darts across all three lanes in one swooping motion. Every other driver that follows begins a circus elephant processional. They simply grab onto their friend's tail (or in this case, car bumper) and follow in a quasi-orderly fashion. Never mind the fact that the leader of the herd failed to acknowledge the other lanes of traffic after his initial lane change.

By the time I come up along the access road, I can clearly see the herd in my way. The elephants float across my lane at about 20 mph and form a barricade that hinders my successful journey toward the stoplight that they are all desperate to avoid. Not one of them appears to spend a moment in that first lane checking their rearview mirrors before proceeding. Instead, they are engaging in a group norm to stake out an imaginary freeway onramp in the middle of my three-lane access road.

This presents a dilemma for me. On a good day, when all goes well at the house getting ready for work, I simply slow down and yield to the vehicles crossing my path, just as I would for a herd of seemingly delirious elephants who don't know any better. They mean no harm. Best to let them go and I will just wait. That's on a good day.

On a bad day, every bone in my body says, "Stay the course. It's my lane; I own it." This is America, and roadway lanes are prime real estate. In America, drivers are not allowed to dart in front of you, especially when you're traveling at a dominant 50 mph and they're piddling along at 20. They need to wait for the lane to clear. So what if they can't make their first onramp to the freeway? It's my lane—back off, Jack.

Here's what typically happens next on my less-than-stellar mornings: I take the center lane at a comfortable (and legal!) 50 mph, cover my horn in anticipation, and steam ahead. As I get close to the mergers—who, in fact, are not looking in their rearview mirrors or over their shoulders at all—I slam on my brakes and honk my horn, cackling like a possessed man in response to their startled, shocked faces. They are surprised by my presence. Interestingly, they decide now is a good time to use their rearview mirrors as they ponder, "Where did that guy come from?"

In this situation, there is an unquestionable duty to mitigate. It would be absurd for me to try to teach those reckless elephants a lesson by not yielding to their dangerous access-road shenanigans. After all, I want to get to work alive just like they do. So I mitigate, I slow down and let them mosey on over to the freeway entrance. There is no justification for me to mow them down because they are engaging in at-risk or even reckless behaviors. When I see or anticipate such a mistake or behavior, I have a moral obligation as a driver to attempt to mitigate the potential harm. In such times of life, we have no right to further contribute to a potential adverse outcome. We have a duty to mitigate.

A Complicated Mess?

Here's the reality: we owe an overwhelming number of duties to those around us and they to us. We might even add in a few duties we believe we owe ourselves, or for some, a duty to a higher being, a higher force. These duties take the form described in the last five chapters:

The Duty to Produce Outcomes
The Duty to Follow Procedural Rules
The Duty to Avoid Causing Unjustifiable Risk or Harm
The Duty to Save
The Duty to Mitigate

Put simply, it's about "doing the right thing." Our job is to navigate through the many duties that face us, trying always to do the right thing. An easy set of instructions, if life were simple. For most of us, doing the right thing is not always so easy. Competing duties always seem to make decision-making difficult. And then there's our human fallibility.

Sometimes it will be human error that keeps us from

doing the right thing. Perhaps we inadvertently run a stop sign. We might have had our eyes focused on the road, radio off, no distractions. Yet, in the moment, our mind simply does not register the stop sign. Without any risky behavioral choices, we are still going to make mistakes. We don't choose them—they happen to us.

Sometimes we will not do the right thing because we drift into at-risk behavior. As humans, we are always looking for quicker, easier ways to navigate through the many duties we daily face. So, we look for short cuts. Perhaps, as a child, it was hiding toys and trash under the bed as a means to make the bedroom look visually clean. Somehow, we thought it would meet the technical expectations of a clean room, while allowing more time to play with friends. As adults, we're taught to have our hands on the steering wheel at nine and three, yet we find ourselves calling, texting, eating, even dressing while en route to our destination—all with an eye toward saving time. It's not doing the right thing; yet, we convince ourselves that we're in a safe place, that the behavior we're engaged in is necessary to meet all our other equally important duties.

Sometimes we will not do the right thing because the pull of one value causes us to disregard what we know is a higher duty, a higher value. Perhaps the draw of the party is enough to convince us that driving intoxicated is a risk we're willing to take—that it's OK to gamble with other people's lives. It's reckless; we even recognize it for what it is: the conscious disregard of a substantial and unjustifiable risk. Many of us (hopefully only in our more reckless, younger years) made just this choice, convinced that the risk wasn't as great as everybody said. After all, we had made it home intoxicated without any mishap on more than one occasion, as had many or all of our friends.

Finally, we may not do the right thing by knowingly or purposely harming others. Murder, theft, arson—most of what we call crime—fall into this last category.

Wouldn't it be nice if life were designed so that doing the right thing was also the easy thing? But this underestimates the complexity of life, the competing values with which we're faced each day. What kept the maintenance technicians at American Airlines from following the safer engine change procedures laid out in the DC-10 maintenance manuals? What kept the bystanders watching Kitty Genovese's brutal attack from calling the police, or attempting in some way to intervene? What prevented the emergency room staff at Ravenswood Hospital from giving aide to Christopher Sercye?

The technicians at American Airlines thought they were doing a good thing: improving efficiency in a manner that appeared to them to be safe. The bystanders in Genovese's death probably knew they were not doing the right thing, but perhaps feared for their own safety. The emergency room personnel at Ravenswood who were aware of Sercye's condition as he lay outside the hospital surely felt angst about their failure to help. Yet a rule is a rule: no one leaves the ER to render aide.

Life is complex. The duties, the expectations, the responsibilities seem endless. They overlap in a manner that makes much of the world appear as one vast, gray area. If I meet this duty now, then I can't meet that other equally important duty. When my youngest son was two years old, I envied his life—it was a carefree existence that only required him to live in the moment.

For adults, though, life is all about duties. It's the duty to avoid causing unjustifiable risk or harm that is the controlling obligation. The rules we create as humans are intended to support and give guidance around this duty. When the rules we create conflict with doing the right thing—it's doing the right thing that controls. It's not simple, it's not easy, but it is clear. Do the right thing—that's the duty owed. That's hopefully what our parents taught us. We will make mistakes; it's part of our DNA. That said, our job is to focus on making the safest possible choices, always trying to do the right thing.

So where are we at today in our adult world? Is doing the right thing actually the duty? Consider this: the National Highway Traffic Safety Administration reported that in 2007 an estimated 12,998 people died in alcohol-impaired traffic crashes involving a driver with an illegal blood alcohol content (.08 or greater). These deaths constituted 31.7 percent of the 41,059 total traffic fatalities in 2007.

This statistic alone should tell us that drinking alcohol and driving is not doing the right thing. Clearly, this behavioral choice results in an unjustifiable increase in the risk of harm. Need more statistics? Here are some gathered from LearnAboutAlcoholism.com:

In a country of 300 million people, one-third of all Americans will be involved in drunk driving accidents at some point in their life time.

Drunk drivers are less likely to wear their safety belts than sober drivers, putting themselves at greater risk for injury in the event of an accident.

Someone is injured in an alcohol-related car accident approximately every sixty seconds.

Someone dies in an alcohol-related car accident approximately every forty minutes.

Sixty percent of all teen deaths in car accidents are alcohol-related.

Drunk driving car accidents cost the U.S. an average of $114 billion annually.

If you weren't convinced before reading those statistics, it should be fairly easy for us to agree on at least one point: drinking and driving will never qualify as doing the right thing. Drinking and driving does not happen by mistake; the person who chooses to drink without making arrangements for getting home prior to being impaired by alcohol chooses recklessness.

So how do we deal with drunk driving in the U.S.? Consider the state of Wisconsin's approach. Under

Wisconsin law, a first drunk driving conviction is not even a crime and gets no jail time; it is classified simply as a civil infraction resulting in fines ranging from $150 to $300 plus a $365 surcharge with a suspension or revocation of the person's driver's license for six to nine months. Under Wisconsin law, the second, third, and fourth drunk driving convictions are misdemeanors, meaning they are punishable by less than a year in prison. Under Wisconsin law, it is not until a fifth drunk driving conviction that the people of Wisconsin are willing to make it a felony, punishable by more than a year in prison.

OK, we get the idea. It's bad, but not that bad. No three strikes and you're out here—in Wisconsin you get five! Well, that is, unless you hurt someone. In Wisconsin, if you cause the death of another person or an unborn child by operating a vehicle while under the influence of alcohol, you may be charged with a class D felony, punishable by a fine up to $100,000 and imprisonment up to twenty-five years.

Yep, it's sort of about doing the right thing. Well, it's really about doing what you want unless, of course, you harm another person. It's the harm, not the choice to drive drunk, that gets you in trouble. As long as you're lucky enough not to kill anyone, Wisconsin allows you a felony pass for your first four convictions. However, if you're unlucky enough to have killed a family on your first drunk driving conviction, you'll be imprisoned for up to twenty-five years and face a fine of up to $100,000. Does anyone think this concept is flawed? Does this make any sense? Is the potential risk any different in these two scenarios? Should our response to drunk driving be based on who is unlucky enough to make the mistake when they are driving drunk?

There is a profound Whack-a-Mole message here, one that can teach us about our culture's notion of duty. We live in a no harm, no foul society. So long as the mole doesn't pop his head out of his hole, we're all OK. If I'm willing to exercise my individual freedom by taking the risk of driving intoxicated, and I can make it home without killing anyone, that should validate my decision to drive intoxicated.

We can't just pick on the state of Wisconsin. Many states follow similar (il)logic in setting drunk driving penalties. It's a logic that permeates other areas of life, even high-risk industries. It's the doctor who argues he can ignore universal safety protocols because they don't apply to him, because he himself has not yet caused harm. It's the pilot who insists on doing his pre-flight check from memory or the aviation maintenance mechanic who checks for cracks with a flashlight because dragging those huge, high wattage lights closer to the aircraft is such a pain. It's the Wall Street bankers who engage in riskier and riskier deals that are ignored as long as 401k's continue to rise in value. It's the mom who talks on a cell phone while driving her kids to school, justifying the behavior based upon the fact that she hasn't gotten into an accident yet.

It *is* about doing the right thing. Somewhere along the way, we transitioned into a society that says, "Do what you want...as long as you don't hurt anyone." In America, perhaps there's an underlying devotion to our strongly guarded freedom to do what we want. Only here, we've extended that freedom to take unreasonable risks with the lives of other people. We often hear the refrain, "But it was legal," or "It wasn't against the law." Or we hear, "But I didn't hurt anyone," or "Nothing bad happened." Seems like a pretty low standard. Perhaps our simple test should be this: "Was it the right thing to do"?

Mothers Against Drunk Driving had it right. After all, they didn't call themselves Mothers Against Drivers Who Have Killed Another Person While Drunk. Or, Mothers for Driving Drunk as Long as No One is Hurt. They focused on the behavior—rightly so. It is about doing the right thing— and when we say that, it's about doing the right thing in the systems we design and in the behavioral choices we make. Beyond that, we'll all simply have to live with the errors and the adverse events that result. The duties lie within the former, our sympathies extend to those involved in the latter.

Tommy's Volcano

It's about doing the right thing to avoid harm. It's also about doing the right thing when things do go wrong. Interestingly, what we do after adverse events will have a large impact on our ability to prevent adverse events in the first place. Remember what Dr. Lucian Leape testified to Congress: the single greatest impediment to error prevention in the medical industry is that we punish people for making mistakes. What we do in response to our human fallibility will directly influence our shared safety, security, and prosperity.

Flashback to seventh grade science class. We all had to do a project. Study something, then build a prop, something physical that went along with our research. Then, when all the projects were complete, we'd get together and have a little science fair.

At this point in my life, I can't even remember what my project was about because it was clouded by Tommy's project. Tommy studied volcanoes, so he built this very cool plaster volcano with pluming smoke created by dry ice. It was magical. I was so intrigued, so engrossed by it that I just had to touch it. Two days before the big science fair, I reached out and touched Tommy's volcano. Not in any malicious way, but just to feel it.

That's when it happened. As my hands carefully contacted his volcano, the plaster cracked. That poor volcano shattered right there in front of me as I was talking to Tommy. I said I was sorry, but Tommy just stood there and shifted his eyes between me and his volcano, which now lay in a heap. Tommy would be graded on his volcano and at this point it was basically inoperable. It looked like the pieces of a broken dish. I'm not sure anyone could even recognize it as a volcano. The deed was done, and I—I was the culprit.

Now Tommy was not about to lose all his hard work and risk a failing grade because of a friend. He told the teacher, who offered a reasonable remedy. I would have to rebuild Tommy's volcano in two days. Tommy would still provide the dry ice; I just had to replace the volcano itself. The problem is that I did not have any experience working with plaster. Salt dough, yes. But, plaster? No.

I felt terrible. So terrible that I did not want anyone beyond Tommy, the teacher, and myself to know what had happened. I was embarrassed. So, I arrived home after school announcing to my mom that I had to build a second project prop—a salt dough volcano painted brown with red molten fire colored around the top. It would have to be done in two days.

I'm not sure whether my mom knew what was going on or whether my teacher even contacted my parents. I just remember building the volcano with the constant thought that I was hiding something. It was a miserable forty-eight hours. I had made a mistake in touching something that was much more fragile than I ever anticipated and I broke it. I was sick to my stomach.

When I arrived back at school with the replacement volcano, Tommy was not impressed. The salt dough was never going to look as good as the plaster, and to add insult to injury, my salt dough did not set as I had hoped. My volcano seemed to droop. It was slowly getting smaller at the top and larger at the bottom. Had it been a week until the science fair, my replacement volcano would have likely resembled a pancake.

I am not sure what I learned at the time from this mishap. I barely touched Tommy's volcano, but the adverse outcome was there—and I was technically the cause. I wasn't trying to do the wrong thing when I touched that volcano, yet I was subsequently strapped with days of lies, cover-up, and guilt. In the end, all I produced was a slumping cone well short of Tommy's awesome, albeit fragile, plaster volcano.

At the time, I felt confident that I could prevent this from happening again. Yet, at the same time, what happened after the broken volcano was an absolute train wreck. I was mortified, sick to my stomach. I couldn't tell my parents out of sheer embarrassment, and perhaps out of fear they would restrict my activities. You know, bad outcome must mean bad actor. Bad actor means being grounded for a while. Even though my only transgression was to touch a plaster volcano that was already teetering on the edge of breaking apart, I thought the end of my life was imminent should my parents find out what I had done.

I simply did not have at my disposal the range of remedies that could make this event a healthy experience. Tommy wound up with a sickly volcano, and I wound up feeling sick myself.

In the song "El Condor Pasa," Simon and Garfunkel sing: "I'd rather be a hammer than a nail/Yes I would. If I only could/I surely would." It's no wonder. As a child, the Whack-a-Mole technique had already been deeply instilled in me. I'd done something wrong; it didn't matter if I intended to ruin Tommy's volcano or not—I'd done it. And for days I made myself sick waiting for the whack, for the hammer to fall.

We need societal systems that allow us to do the right thing after an adverse event has occurred. We need a system to learn from adverse events, to help us deter future events. We also need a system to make amends with those who have been harmed, to not let a mistake exact an unnecessary toll on a fellow human being.

We begin with deterrence, the attempt to prevent future adverse events.

Part Four

Deterrence

Perhaps "deterrence" is a bit of a legal word. The goal is to create better outcomes. To do that, we must learn from our mistakes, creating better systems and making better choices as we move forward. The question is, does our current legal system with its goal of deterrence help us do that?

Dings and Whacks

Whether it's the state taking action against a citizen, whether it's an employer taking action against an employee, or whether it's a parent taking action with a child, there are two broad ways of taking "disciplinary" action: dings, and well, whacks. They are different. Dings are not whacks. Whacks are not dings. They are two scientifically distinct categories, as you can probably tell from the technical nature of these words: dings and whacks.

Have you ever received a speeding ticket? That's a ding. No requirement on the part of the police officer to show that you chose to speed. No requirement on the part of the police officer to show you had a reckless disregard for the safety of others. The only requirement is that his radar gun clocked you going faster than the speed limit.

Consider my last speeding ticket. I was leaving the freeway, merging onto a three-lane access road (the same circus-elephant-filled access road discussed earlier). I left the freeway doing 65 mph. By the time I was on the access road, I was still doing 60 mph. The speed limit on this stretch of the access road is 45 mph. Busted. A $150 ticket and the time and expense required taking the driver's education course to keep it off of my driving record and hidden from my insurance carrier.

As soon as I received my ticket, I called the office on my hands-free mobile phone. "I'll be in the office in about ten minutes. I got a ticket for speeding, doing 60 in a 45 on the Central Expressway access road."

It was a ding. No social condemnation. No significant feelings of embarrassment. Yes, I was doing the wrong thing, both legally and toward those around me. Sixty miles per hour on the access road was not the right thing to do. That said, I was relatively open with my colleagues and family about what had happened. I did not live up to expectations, and I got dinged.

Whacks are different. Whacks come with societal condemnation. Whacks come with blame; whacks come with a message that the human at issue has fallen far short of societal expectations. Drunk driving would be a good example. Had I been drunk when I received my speeding ticket, it's not likely I would have been so open about it when I arrived at work. I would feel shame, I would be embarrassed. And society would rightfully stand in judgment.

Just look at the rash of current Hollywood stars who have been caught driving drunk. We respond differently—both emotionally and legally—to any incident of drunk driving than we do to a racecar driver caught speeding. In the case of drunk driving, we demand a whack. Whacks are meant to send a very strong signal to both the perpetrator and to society as a whole: we do not tolerate this behavior. Unless our racecar driver is driving 90 mph on a residential street, we're all comfortable with a ding in response to his or her speeding. Dings are the nominal fines, the gentle reminders that let us know that we are outside of prescribed bounds.

For the most part, we should accept with little complaint the dings that society imposes on us. It's the whacks that have become particularly problematic. From government regulator to corporate employer, if you live in the modern world, you're likely to get caught up in the game of whacks, the game of Whack-a-Mole.

Management Whacking

I have never met a person who entered management out of a desire to fire employees. It's definitely painful for the employee and generally painful for the boss. Dealing with employees, at least the negative side of employee relations, is a cost of doing business.

Imagine yourself as the station manager at a national airline. You manage, in part, those ground crew members that passengers, sitting in their window seats, see working around the aircraft. Baggage loaders, fuelers, deicers, lavatory service employees.

An aircraft is expensive, costing anywhere from $50 to $200 million each. The job of the baggage handler on the ground, in addition to carefully loading your baggage in the belly of the aircraft so as not to destroy it, is also not to damage the airplane. Don't hit the airplane with the belt loader that moves bags into the belly of the aircraft. Don't hit the airplane with the fuel service truck. Don't ram the aircraft with the jet bridge. In aviation, they call it ground damage. Modern aircraft are made of aluminum and composites—and they are expensive to repair. One hit to an engine by an errant belt loader may cause more than $100,000 in damage.

Wow. With those kinds of damage costs, you might assume ground damage to airplanes is pretty rare. You'd be wrong. Aircraft are hit on a regular basis. At some bases, the rate can be as high as one hit of the aircraft for every 1,000 flights. At a major hub for an airline, there can be a ground damage event just about every day. It costs the airline industry *billions* of dollars each year.

Fortunately, lawyers and human resources departments have developed guidance for these circumstances. It's called the "progressive discipline policy." Written to support the correct working relationship between employer and employee, in practice they are often more about classifying anything the employee has done that causes damage under the category of prohibited conduct. Involved in a ground damage event? Suffer the wrath of the progressive discipline policy. Simple really.

What follows is an actual, though de-identified, disciplinary policy of a large U.S. airline given to me several years ago. It's a mishap disciplinary policy that guides airline managers on treatment of employees who damage equipment or harm another person. Many of you may have never seen the disciplinary policy of the company where you work—and that's probably a good thing. They're not pretty. They are typically one-sided, written by the organization to protect itself. As you read through this policy's provisions, consider what it says about human fallibility. Does it allow the employee to be human or does it require more-than-human, perfect performance?

Progressive Discipline Policy

This policy of progressive discipline is mandatory for all employees responsible for causing a mishap. The purpose of this policy is to provide a consistent corporate disciplinary policy. In order to ensure consistent discipline, any deviation from this policy must be discussed with Employee Relations prior to taking action.

1. Employee(s) involved in, or witness to, a mishap (regardless of the severity), who fail to report the incident are subject to termination.
2. Employee(s) tested positive for drugs or alcohol who are involved in a mishap will be terminated immediately.
3. Mishaps which are the result of a violation of established Corporate Policy and Procedures will result in five days suspension of the employee involved without pay, for the first offense and termination of employment for the second offense in an eighteen month period.
4. Any employee acting with purposeful actions and conduct motivated by a malicious or discriminatory purpose (harassment, horseplay) will be terminated.
5. Any employee involved in any mishap resulting from a judgment error but who notifies management in a

timely fashion (within 10 minutes of the mishap) will be disciplined as follows:

a) For the first offense in an eighteen month period, a letter of discipline will be retained in the employee's personnel file for eighteen months, AND the employee will receive five days off without pay.

b) Any employee involved in two mishaps will be terminated.

c) Any employee involved in a mishap in the past eighteen months is not eligible for a promotion or temporary upgrade.

d) Anyone who knowingly assigns an employee to a position for which he/she is not adequately trained, or exposes him/her to an obvious risk, or intentionally conceals, obscures, or misrepresents information associated with a mishap will be terminated.

6. Prior to the employee's return to work, the most senior management person in the station/department will meet with the employee and discuss the mishap and their return to work. Documentation of the counseling session, along with a signed statement from the management employee, will be retained in the employee's personnel file for eighteen months. A copy will be sent to the Safety Department for review.

7. Mishaps which are the result of negligence will not be tolerated; any employee that negligently performs their duties and causes a mishap will be terminated.

So what does this policy really say? It's written as plain as an attorney can write it, yet in many ways it evades comprehension. It looks legal; it looks scary. Within the policy, there are a few provisions that rightly prohibit crimes of intent. That is, lying, drug use, failure to report. These things clearly cross the line, with the employee being not only aware that his or her actions were misaligned with the values of the airline but that they fell under the employee's duty to produce an outcome.

There are several provisions, however, that promote the Whack-a-Mole approach. The first is this:

5. Any employee involved in any mishap resulting from a judgment error but who notifies management in a timely fashion (within 10 minutes of the mishap) will be disciplined as follows:
   a) For the first offense in an eighteen month period, a letter of discipline will be retained in the employee's personnel file for eighteen months, AND the employee will receive five days off without pay.
   b) Any employee involved in two mishaps will be terminated.

Whack. These are not dings. These are whacks. Yet, the

reference here is to a judgment error, a human error in most instances—similar to misjudging your driving speed and inadvertently running a red light. The first offense gets you five days off of work without pay; the second gets you fired. It's a provision that appears to make human error a very serious offense. Two strikes and you're out. Given the penalties, employees are unlikely to volunteer that they made a "judgment" error. Beyond these provisions, perhaps the most problematic policy provision is the last:

7. Mishaps which are the result of negligence will not be tolerated; any employee that negligently performs their duties and causes a mishap will be terminated.

Negligence, in the law, is no different than human error in the everyday world. Anyone who makes a mistake and causes a mishap will be terminated. That's quite the deterrent. But a deterrent to what? The human being who makes a mistake is not very amenable to the deterrent, as the human error, by definition, would not have been intended. Yes, the employee might have made some bad choices, but those could be identified as at-risk or reckless behaviors, distinguished from the inadvertent and unintentional human error.

This policy surely stifles the reporting of errors, (assuming employees have actually read the policy). Recognizing that behind each error are the lessons to be learned that might prevent the next, possibly more serious mishap, safety advocates in high-consequence industries are trying to get employees to report, not hide, their errors. Policies like the one shown above simply act to deter open communication, striking an unproductive tension between the need to learn and the need to hold individuals accountable for their actions.

As you might imagine, with policies like this not everyone who strikes an aircraft with a belt loader feels compelled to come forward. Predictably, most damage to the aircraft is not reported by the person causing it. Airlines spend substantial sums of money for dent monitoring programs to detect and monitor dents on the exterior surface of their aircraft. They routinely find new dents on the exterior of their multi-million dollar aircraft, just as we might find a new dent on our car. The problem in the airline industry is that these dents are on the shell of the aircraft, the shell that holds the pressurized environment for its passengers. We should feel safer when our airline's damage policy encourages the reporting of mishaps, rather than merely threatening to fire the employee who makes a mistake.

Also at issue with this progressive discipline policy is that it focuses only on the mishap itself. It focuses solely on who is to blame when a mishap occurs. It seems to ignore the fact that risky behaviors should be addressed *before* those behaviors lead to harm. This policy waits for the mishap and then looks back. The better disciplinary policy addresses the behavior before the behavior causes a mishap.

Surely we can create a disciplinary policy that allows the station manager to take action when he sees reckless behavior, while also promoting an open learning culture around more basic human fallibility. The policy provisions, without the legalese, might look like this:

> You are a fallible human being, susceptible to human error and behavioral drift. As your employer, we must design systems around you in recognition of that fallibility. When errors do occur, you must raise your hand to allow the organization to learn. When you make a mistake, you will be consoled. When you drift into a risky place, believing that you are still safe, we will coach you. When you knowingly put others in harm's way, we will take appropriate disciplinary action.

Around the world in high-consequence industries, organizations are moving in this direction. Many are abandoning punitive disciplinary policies that serve only to deter reporting of hazards, while at the same time offering little help to the individual who has drifted into risky choices. It's called a Just Culture. It's the middle ground between a highly punitive system and a system where no one is accountable at all (the "blame free" system of justice). The Just Culture embraces the console, coach, and punish model attached to the human error, at-risk behavior, and reckless behavior. For the manager, it's a path that allows employees to report their errors, to be truthful about their at-risk behaviors, while still holding them accountable through disciplinary action for their reckless actions.

It's a better path than Whack-a-Mole.

State Whacking

Every professional practice has its own standard of care. The regulatory framework recognizes this. We create standards to enforce minimal competencies among those to whom we entrust our lives—from firefighters and pilots, to nurses and nuclear power plant operators. Consider the pilot who crosses an active runway without authorization or flies to an altitude not assigned by air traffic control. There are specific provisions in the regulations to address such deviations. There is also the general duty clause, the standard of care if you will. For a pilot, it's the "careless or reckless" rule in the Federal Aviation Regulations (FAR). This FAR reads, in part, as follows:

FAR 91.13 Careless or reckless operation.
(a) *Aircraft operations for the purpose of air navigation.* No person may operate an aircraft in a careless or reckless manner so as to endanger the life or property of another.

This is not the type of rule that says, "Stop at all stop

signs," and provides explicit notice of the duty to produce an outcome. The careless or reckless rule is instead about breach. That is, what will we do with you when you don't live up to standards? It is a rule that looks at the potential harm to the life or property of another, and lets you know what intent toward that harm gets you in trouble.

This rule prohibits "careless or reckless" operation of an aircraft that endangers life or property. Reckless behavior, as discussed earlier, involves the conscious disregard of a substantial and unjustifiable risk. It is putting life or property in harm's way with the knowledge of substantial and unjustifiable risk. Technically, it means that any reasonable person would have to know the risk exists and that taking the risk is absolutely the wrong thing to do.

Obviously, it is reasonable that we expect that our pilot will not knowingly put us in harm's way. We clearly don't want reckless pilots flying for our nation's airlines. The problem arises with the word "careless." Careless, as a legal term, is quite different from reckless behavior. In fact, the term "careless" is legally interpreted to mean simple human error. Read what a National Transportation Safety Board (NTSB) administrative law judge had to say in the case of a pilot who was appealing a seemingly unjust enforcement action by the FAA:

> "As far as I am concerned, when I say 'careless' I am not talking about any kind of 'reckless' operation of an aircraft, but simply the most basic form of simple human error or omission that the Board has used in these cases

in its definition of 'carelessness.' In other words, a simple absence of the due care required under the circumstances, that is, a simple act of omission, or simply 'ordinary negligence,' a human mistake."

The careless and reckless rule clearly informs pilots that perfection is the standard. If they are less than perfect, that is, if they make a mistake, the FAA is coming after them—Whack-a-Mole. For the FAA, this is a good, tough stand. It makes Congress happy, it makes the media happy, it makes everyone happy. The problem is that it makes air travel less safe.

The FAA's Game of Cat and Mouse

You're going to make mistakes in life. Learn from them. It could be the most important step in response to human fallibility: to learn. If we could learn why the mistake or at-risk behavioral choice occurred, we might then know how to prevent it from happening again. The FAA knows this, and as a regulatory agency it has led the way in creating safety reporting systems. It has always known the importance of a good learning culture. This leads us to the problem at hand: reconciling two incompatible views. The FAA can either hold airmen to an expectation of perfection or learn from the mistakes that airmen make—they really can't do both.

Let's imagine the scenario of running a red light while driving your car. You run the light because you're distracted by something alongside the road. Or perhaps you were driving a bit slower than normal and consequently miscalculated your ability to get through the upcoming light before it turned red.

A police officer spots the infraction. Lights whirl, siren shrieks. You're busted. The police officer approaches you and asks some basic questions. "No, I didn't realize I ran a red light," you say, trying your best to look surprised by the whole encounter. "Well, irrespective of your error, I am going to have to write you a ticket." As the officer begins the paperwork, you ask permission to reach into your glove compartment. You pull out your get-out-of-jail-free card, which entitles you to one pass from enforcement action; the only requirement is that you give the police officer a written safety report outlining the reasons you ran the light. The police officer grimaces, reluctantly accepts your write-up and forgoes any ticket. Safety is served, and you're off the hook—at least for this offense.

The Aviation Safety Reporting System

If you are a pilot flying in the U.S., you actually do get to use the get-out-of-jail-free card. It's found within the Aviation Safety Reporting System (ASRS), a program administered by the National Aeronautics and Space Administration (NASA) on behalf of the FAA. It began in 1976 as a critical means to gather otherwise inaccessible safety information.

Why create such a system? Because of an entrenched code of silence: what happens in the cockpit stays in the cockpit. The FAA is chartered with both promoting aviation and keeping it safe. To keep aviation safe, the FAA must know where the current system is failing. The FAA needs to see those near misses—the precursors to the accidents they are charged to prevent. If the FAA had the opportunity to learn about pilot mistakes, it could investigate and understand why they had occurred. Safety would be served.

So why would the average pilot not pick up the phone and just call the local FAA inspector? By sharing the story of the last altitude deviation, other pilots, air traffic controllers, and aircraft manufacturers could learn how to prevent potential disasters. Why not report? For the same reason you won't pick up the phone to inform the police of the last red light you inadvertently ran. Because the pilot, like you (I hope), is not crazy. Who in their right mind would call the police on themselves and face potential sanction—even if it were for the benefit of society?

It's that old "careless or reckless operation of an aircraft" rule. You know, make a mistake as a pilot and it's time for Whack-a-Mole. The FAA's enforcement guidelines provide that the FAA can either impose a financial penalty (fine) or pull the certificate of the pilot who made a mistake that endangered the life or property of another. Now, for a private pilot, pulling his certification is only the end of a hobby. For a commercial pilot, it's the end of a career.

Recognizing the significant limitations of Whack-a-Mole to encourage pilots to come forward to report their errors in the interests of safety, the FAA created ASRS, essentially aviation's get-out-of-jail-free card. Believing that the value in punishing the human error was outweighed by the value in learning from the mistake, the FAA created ASRS as an enforcement-related incentive, a safe haven of sorts for pilots to report their errors without fear of FAA sanction.

It's an enforcement-related incentive because the FAA never changed the underlying rule for either commercial or private pilots—human error is still against the rules and considered actionable. If a pilot does not meet the standard of perfection, then the FAA can fine or pull the pilot's certificate to fly. This disciplinary stick remains in effect today.

The carrot is ASRS. The FAA apparently wants the pilot to be afraid of making a mistake (the stick) yet it also wants to learn about the mistake when it does occur, introducing the need for the carrot. The ASRS provides the incentive to report, but with restrictions. After all, not everyone has the same definition of the word "mistake." The FAA could not allow an intoxicated pilot to use the get-of-jail-free card, just as a parent has to draw the line on what childhood mistakes can be reported with impunity. In Advisory Circular 00-46D, the FAA stipulates:

> "The filing of a report with NASA concerning an incident or occurrence involving a violation of the…[Federal Aviation Regulations] is considered by the FAA to be indicative of a constructive attitude. Such an attitude will tend to prevent future violations. Accordingly, although a finding of a violation may be

made, neither a civil penalty nor certificate suspension will be imposed if:

1. the violation was inadvertent and not deliberate;
2. the violation did not involve a criminal offense, or accident, or action under section 49 U.S.C. Section 44709 which discloses a lack of qualification or competency, which is wholly excluded from this policy;
3. the person has not been found in any prior FAA enforcement action to have committed a violation of 49 U.S.C. Subtitle VII, or any regulation promulgated there for a period of 5 years prior to the date of the occurrence; and
4. the person proves that, within 10 days after the violation, he or she completed and delivered or mailed a written report of the incident or occurrence to NASA under ASRS. "

So what do you notice in the guidance? First, it's a no harm, no foul system. If you've had an accident, no use of the get-out-of-jail-free card. Second, the violation has to be inadvertent. You cannot knowingly violate a Federal Aviation Regulation and then attempt to use the card. Third, you only get to use the get-out-of-jail-free card once every five years. Fourth, the error cannot be criminal, whatever that term means. Lastly, you have to send the report to NASA, the key to the learning process.

So what did the FAA create? They start with a rule that

aircraft pilots must be perfect, killing any hope for the open reporting of safety events and near misses. In response, they find that they must now create a get-out-of-jail-free system to provide "immunity" to those who come forward to report their errors (so long as they only make one mistake in any five year period).

The ASRS enforcement-related incentive might remind you of a number of television crime dramas. You know, where the police arrest the small time drug offender with a few ounces of marijuana in his possession and offer the offender immunity if he'll rat out his presumably bigger supplier. They'll give immunity to the criminal in order to achieve their larger goal of significantly reducing the amount of drugs in the community. That's what the ASRS system is doing—allowing the pilot to rat on himself. Like the drug dealer, he's a wrongdoer; but we'll allow him to trade information for immunity, knowing that his safety report is the key to operational improvements.

There is one critical difference, however, between our small-time, drug-dealing criminal and our pilot: intent. The drug dealer is not dealing drugs by mistake. His choice to sell drugs can't be called human error. Our drug dealer chose to commit an illegal act, fully knowing the act was well outside social expectations. The pilot, on the other hand, did not choose the human error; yet, in offering him immunity through the ASRS enforcement-related incentive, the FAA treats him the same as the criminal. How? By keeping the underlying rule that requires pilots to be perfect.

Perhaps it's just a matter of perspective. One perspective

believes that it makes sense to demand perfection and then engage with wrongdoers and offer immunity if they come forward to admit when they are not perfect. The other perspective believes it's more effective not to expect perfection in the first place. It believes we should embrace our fallibility and make reporting our errors an expectation rather than an illicit trade between a wrongdoer and the regulator who's out to get them.

The Good News at the FAA

Fifty years ago commercial aviation experienced a fatal airplane accident rate on the order of one accident for every 20,000 departures. Today the commercial aviation fatal accident rate in the U.S. is about one accident for every 8 million departures, a 99.75 percent drop in the accident rate. As an industry, commercial aviation learned to use the engineering controls of barriers, redundancy, and recovery to reduce the rate of error and create more error-tolerant systems. Aircraft designers learned to design in recognition of human fallibility.

Asking pilots simply to take more care was not going to make the difference. It was designing in recognition of human fallibility that would make the difference, done not by the airplane manufacturers, airlines, or regulators in isolation nor in an adversarial mode—but in a spirit of shared responsibility and partnership. Yes, there were those in aviation who wanted (and continue to want) their pound of flesh whenever an adverse event occurs, but we still found ways to design around the predictably fallible pilot, the predictably fallible technician, and the predictably fallible cabin crew. With thousands of lives on the line, we chose to design in recognition of the inevitable, predictable human error.

The FAA's top safety program for the last decade has been a partnership between labor (the airmen), the airline, and the FAA. Rather than playing a traditional game of "cat and mouse"—with the FAA referring to the airline and their employees as "violators," and airlines and labor sharing as little as possible with the punitive regulator—these groups now work collaboratively to improve safety using a new model: the Aviation Safety Action Program (ASAP).

In these programs, the FAA now has visibility within the airlines to view safety reports submitted by pilots, dispatchers, mechanics, and flight attendants. Since its inception at American Airlines in 1994, the FAA has approved over 170 ASAP programs throughout the U.S. ASAP programs have demonstrated that without this transparency, the FAA would have been otherwise aware of less than one percent of the safety concerns and rule violations reported under the program. The aviation industry and its regulators have proven that there is a better approach to improving safety and reducing risk than the traditional "blame, shame, and punish" approach used in the past. That said, these successful programs are only a step in the right direction. The FAA still has never really looked at its underlying philosophy toward fallible aviators. As much as we design around human error, the FAA still sees human error as "carelessness," warranting enforcement action.

We must continue to change our expectations of each other. Our focus must be less about human error, and more about behavioral choices. Less about blame, and more about learning. Our doctor. Our pilot. Our kid's school bus driver. Ourselves. We're all fallible. We all make mistakes. The question is can we design a system, a culture, a world where we can safely learn from our mistakes—or do we continue with the game of Whack-a-Mole?

Healthcare Whack-a-Mole

OK. I get it. Aviation is relatively safe. Not much to get worked up about.

Consider, then, another profession. Healthcare. Where we kill, by some estimates, 200,000 people *per year* in the U.S. alone. If we wanted a "get tough" regulator, it is in this industry. Surely it is here that we need more individual accountability. We need to root out all the unprofessional doctors, nurses, and other healthcare providers who are killing these 200,000 people each year.

Welcome to Washington State, which has a general provision within its laws that outlines what the state considers to be "unprofessional conduct" for a healthcare provider. Bear with me here. I know that reading a statute is about as much fun as watching paint dry, but it's important that you read it to understand even better what we mean about demanding perfection and punishing human error.

RCW 18.130.180 reads as follows:

Unprofessional Conduct of a Healthcare Provider

The following conduct, acts, or conditions constitute unprofessional conduct for any license holder under the jurisdiction of this chapter:

(1) The commission of any act involving moral turpitude, dishonesty, or corruption...;

(2) Misrepresentation or concealment of a material fact in obtaining a license or in reinstatement thereof;

(3) All advertising which is false, fraudulent, or misleading;

(4) Incompetence, negligence, or malpractice which results in injury to a patient or which creates an unreasonable risk that a patient may be harmed...;

(5) Suspension, revocation, or restriction of the individual's license to practice any health care profession...;

(6) The possession, use, prescription for use, or distribution of controlled substances or legend drugs in any way other than for legitimate or therapeutic purposes...;

(7) Violation of any state or federal statute or administrative rule regulating the profession in question, including any statute or rule defining or establishing standards of patient care or professional conduct or practice;

(8) Failure to cooperate with the disciplining authority...;

(9) Failure to comply with an order issued by the disciplining authority or a stipulation for informal disposition entered into with the disciplining authority;

(10) Aiding or abetting an unlicensed person to practice when a license is required;

(11) Violations of rules established by any health agency;

(12) Practice beyond the scope of practice as defined by law or rule;

(13) Misrepresentation or fraud in any aspect of the conduct of the business or profession;

(14) Failure to adequately supervise auxiliary staff to the extent that the consumer's health or safety is at risk;

(15) Engaging in a profession involving contact with the public while suffering from a contagious or infectious disease involving serious risk to public health;

(16) Promotion for personal gain of any unnecessary or inefficacious drug, device, treatment, procedure, or service;

(17) Conviction of any gross misdemeanor or felony relating to the practice of the person's profession...;

(18) The procuring, or aiding or abetting in procuring, a criminal abortion;

(19) The offering, undertaking, or agreeing to cure or treat disease by a secret method, procedure, treatment, or medicine...;

(20) The willful betrayal of a practitioner-patient privilege as recognized by law;

(21) Violation of chapter 19.68 RCW;

(22) Interference with an investigation or disciplinary proceeding by willful misrepresentation of facts...;

(23) Current misuse of:

(a) Alcohol;

(b) Controlled substances; or

(c) Legend drugs;

(24) Abuse of a client or patient or sexual contact with a client or patient;

(25) Acceptance of more than a nominal gratuity, hospitality, or subsidy offered by a representative or vendor of medical or health-related products or services...

It's a litany of rules. Difficult for the regulator to write, probably incomprehensible to the average healthcare provider.

What is important in this regulation is what the state of Washington is saying about healthcare providers within the state. They are saying that there are only two classes of healthcare providers: 1) professional providers, and 2) unprofessional providers. Unprofessional providers are those who fall under any of the twenty-five provisions listed above in the state's definition of unprofessional conduct. The professional, it would seem, is the provider who does not do any of the things listed above. Sounds simple enough. If you read the provisions closely, most all of the prohibited acts involve a very high level of knowledge on the part of the healthcare provider that they are doing something wrong.

There are a few, however, that cast that wide net, so wide as to encompass even human error. Consider the following provisions:

> (4) Incompetence, negligence, or malpractice which results in injury to a patient or which creates an unreasonable risk that a patient may be harmed...;
>
> (7) Violation of any state or federal statute or administrative rule regulating the profession in question, including any statute or rule defining or establishing standards of patient care or professional conduct or practice;
>
> (11) Violations of rules established by any health agency;

In these three provisions, nothing more than human error is required. That 60 percent national compliance rate with basic standards for hand hygiene? Remember, it's not that the 40 percent who don't comply are always the same people. It's more like every healthcare provider is non-compliant sometime during the week. It could be human error, it could be that the provider didn't know of the rule. Either way, Washington State does not care. Washington State wants its citizens to know that it has set a high standard. And relative to that high standard? Nearly every healthcare provider in the state engages in unprofessional conduct.

I can personally confirm this, having last year visited a hospital in Washington State where I asked approximately 150 providers if they had engaged in unprofessional conduct. Everyone that I could see in the room raised their hand. One hundred percent of those present admitted to having engaged in unprofessional conduct. Astonishing. All they were really admitting to, however, was having made a clinical human error in their career; an act that, by Washington statute, dumps them into the unprofessional conduct bucket.

Yes, many of the provisions of RCW 18.130.180 involve truly unprofessional conduct: sexual misconduct with a patient, embezzlement, falsification of records, stealing drugs from patients. It's the provisions that allow mere human error into the mix that are problematic. It sets an expectation that nobody can meet, it promotes a culture of hiding errors, and ultimately, it negatively impacts the quality of care Washington State residents receive.

Remember again Dr. Leape's testimony before Congress that the single greatest impediment to reducing medical errors is that we punish people for making mistakes. Can you see what he's referring to in the Washington State statute? Can you see the expectation that we have set for healthcare professionals? Perfection is the standard. Don't meet that standard in aviation, and you are called "careless." Don't meet it in healthcare, and you're called "unprofessional." The doctor who makes a simple prescription ordering error is lumped in with the doctor who anesthetizes his patient for the sole purpose of molesting her. Both are unprofessional, both are condemned and face state sanction for their unprofessional conduct. Whack! This is America—and we're proud to be perfect.

While it's not generally fashionable here in the U.S. to think the best practices may lie outside our country, consider what the British have done, specifically, the Civil Aviation Authority (CAA) of the United Kingdom, where they have taken a slightly different approach:

"The Authority gives an assurance that its primary concern is to secure free and uninhibited reporting and that it will not be its policy to institute proceedings in respect of unpremeditated or inadvertent breaches of the law which come to its attention only because they have been reported under the Scheme, except in cases involving dereliction of duty amounting to gross negligence [recklessness]."

In contrast to the Washington State provision that deems human errors themselves to be "unprofessional conduct," the CAA requires that human error events be reported to the Authority for safety analysis. Further, and unique to the CAA approach to managing human error, is the following provision:

"Where a reported occurrence indicated an unpremeditated or inadvertent lapse by an employee, the Authority would expect the employer to act responsibly and to share its view that free and full reporting is the primary aim, and that every effort should be made to avoid action that may inhibit reporting. The CAA, will accordingly, make it known to employers that, except to the extent that action is needed in order to ensure safety, and except in such flagrant circumstances as are described [above], it expects them to refrain from disciplinary or punitive action which might inhibit their staff from duly reporting incidents of which they may have knowledge."

If they are not already doing it, this is the path that regulators should consider in their expectation for individual professionals. The CAA will take action against the reckless airman and will take enforcement action against those who intend to cause harm. It is not a system without accountability; it is a system that balances system accountability with individual accountability.

All regulators should reconsider how they regulate. They should first abandon the no harm, no foul system of accountability. Choices, after all, do matter. We need not wait for harm to use our regulatory power. Second, regulators should look at where they have created expectations of perfection. Perfection cannot be the standard. Third, they should look to where their enforcement practices create unnecessary impediments to learning. Regulators must find an appropriate balance between system and individual accountability. The pendulum, in many cases, has swung too far toward perfection on the part of the individual as the means for obtaining good system performance. That's playing Whack-a-Mole.

How About Making It a Crime?

In the FAA's Aviation Safety Reporting System, one of the exclusions for being able to safely report is that of criminal conduct. If you have engaged in criminal conduct, you cannot be afforded the protections of the ASRS. We have to draw the line somewhere, right? Yes, we can learn from human errors. That's a far cry from letting criminals participate in the learning process with an assurance that we're not coming after them. There we cannot go. Right?

Julie Thao, Joseph Lepore, and Jan Paladino

Julie Thao was a nurse at St Mary's Medical Center in Madison, Wisconsin. On July 5, 2006, Thao was caring for a 16-year-old young woman in labor. The mother-to-be had a strep infection, leading the doctor to order penicillin to protect the baby from infection. As asserted in the criminal complaint, Thao took a second medication out of the locked storage so that she could show the patient what the actual medication, the penicillin, would look like. Through a series of errors, this second medication (Bupivacaine) was administered to the patient instead of the desired penicillin. Within five minutes of administering the Bupivacaine, the patient was in seizure and dying. This event led the Wisconsin Department of Justice to file a criminal complaint against Thao. If found guilty of the class H felony, Thao faced punishment of a fine not to exceed $25,000 or imprisonment not to exceed six years, or both.

Approximately two months later, while flying over Brazil, two U.S. pilots, Joseph Lepore and Jan Paladino, were involved in the worst aviation accident in Brazil's history. At 37,000 feet, their executive jet clipped the wing of a Gol Airlines 737, sending the 737 spinning out of control, killing all 154 people on board. Similar to Thao, the two pilots found themselves facing criminal charges in Brazil for "a lack of necessary diligence that is expected and required of flight crews."

Both of these events led to public debate. In Wisconsin, the hospital association issued a press release:

> "The Department of Justice's (DOJ) decision to pursue unprecedented criminal charges against a nurse who did not deliberately harm a patient accomplishes nothing other than to compound the anguish of the situation… It makes no sense to add to this tragedy by alleging that this mistake, as upsetting as it was, was more than a human error. And it is cruel to allege that this mistake constituted criminal conduct. By setting a precedent that the DOJ will pursue criminal charges against health care professionals who make unintentional human errors, the

DOJ sends a chilling message to health care professionals now in the state, and to those considering practicing here."

Likewise, in response to the criminal complaint following the aviation accident in Brazil, aviation safety experts have expressed regret. Flight Safety Foundation's Kenneth Quinn said:

"There is a tremendous chilling effect that criminal prosecutions can have on getting people to come forward and admit mistakes. We need to focus not on putting people behind bars, but rather on finding out what went wrong and why, and then to prevent its reoccurrence."

Prosecuting human error is a slippery slope. Few of us would argue against the role of the criminal system in taking care of those who intend to cause harm to another. The important question is whether we should be using the criminal system to exact justice for human errors that were not intended by the human beings involved. Should we criminally prosecute the father who inadvertently left his child in the car rather than dropping him off at daycare? Should we have criminally prosecuted Thao, Lepore, and Paladino?

Morissette v. United States, 342 U.S. 246 (1952)

In December 1948, William Morissette went deer hunting in an inactive bombing range in a sparsely populated area of Michigan. In this range, spent bomb casings had been cleared away into piles that were exposed to the weather and eventually rusted away. On this trip, Morissette did not get a deer. To help cover his expenses, he loaded about three tons of spent casings into his truck and sold them as scrap for a total of $84. To his surprise, I am sure, Morissette was criminally indicted under 18 U.S. Code 641, which provides that "whoever embezzles, steals, purloins, or knowingly converts" U.S. property is punishable by fine and imprisonment.

What made this case important to U.S. legal history is that the jury was essentially instructed to ignore Morissette's intent and focus simply on his actions in converting U.S. property. The reason this case went all the way to the U.S. Supreme Court was essentially the same issue that was at hand in the case of the Wisconsin nurse and the U.S. pilots. Did Morissette have criminal intent? Was evil intent required for him to be found guilty of a crime? Yes, we understand that murder and other high-intent activities deserve criminal penalty, but what about a human mistake?

In this case, now more than five decades old, the Supreme Court sketched the expansion of criminal actions into the realm of human error. In this case, Justice Robert H. Jackson traced the defining elements of a criminal. Jackson wrote that our long history of criminal law required two elements: *actus rea* and *mens rea*, the evil hand and the evil meaning mind. Since the origins of English common law, this combination of the evil hand and the evil mind has been the centerpiece of criminal law. Ask anyone on the street to define the word criminal and they will include a requirement for some level of evil intent—the intent to cause harm. This is why many of us find the criminal indictments against Thao, Lepore, and Paladino to be unsettling. We do not believe these individuals had any evil intent to harm. Rather, they were merely trying to do their job.

Writing for the majority, Jackson addressed the requirement for intent in Morissette. He wrote:

> "The contention that an injury can amount to a crime only when inflicted by intention is no provincial or transient notion. It is as universal and persistent in mature systems of law as belief in freedom of the human will and a consequent ability and duty of the normal individual to choose between good and evil. A relation between some mental element and punishment for a harmful act is almost as instinctive as the child's familiar exculpatory, 'But I didn't mean to...' Unqualified acceptance of this doctrine by English common law in the Eighteenth Century was indicated by Blackstone's sweeping statement that to constitute any crime there must first be a 'vicious will.'"

There is something inside us that sees criminal behaviors as being intrinsically tied to evil intent, something that appears lacking in the case of Thao, Lepore, and Paladino. In that 1955 case, however, Jackson went on to describe what had fifty years later put Thao, Lepore, and Paladino in jeopardy—an accelerating tendency to hold individuals responsible for behavior that leads to harm but lacks any ingredient of intent or evil-meaning mind. That is, human error. Justice Jackson referred to these new crimes as public welfare offenses. He spoke of the industrial revolution that exposed many more workers to increasingly powerful and complex mechanisms. He spoke of the advent of automobiles where, through our behaviors, we could cause tremendous harm to one another. He spoke of the wide distribution of goods that would allow errors and harm to propagate at great distance. These industrial advances caused legislatures in the early 1900s to pass laws that no longer required evil intent as a necessary element to be considered crimes. It was the birth of criminal negligence—or to put it in terms relevant to Thao, Lepore, and Paladino, the birth of criminal human error.

The civil, criminal, and regulatory systems are increasingly obscuring the difference between intentional risky choices and inadvertent, predictable human fallibility. The net we cast to catch criminals has now caught those whose only crime is that they are human. In our zeal to exert public control, we've made human error a crime. While punishment is inarguably appropriate for criminals with *actus rea* and *mens rea*, it is counterproductive and serves no purpose for human error or at-risk behavior, which by definition preclude evil intent.

The reality is that mere human error is now criminal in a number of circumstances where public safety is an issue. If our colleague or friend has been convicted of a crime, we can no longer infer that they had evil intent—we can only say that they breached an obligation that our lawmakers chose to categorize as criminal. Jackson recognized the slippery slope we were on when we began criminalizing human error. His judgment said, essentially, that there's a time for a ding and a time for a whack when it comes to punishment. That net we cast to catch criminals may now ensnare well-meaning individuals who have made predictably human mistakes. Casting the net this broadly and bringing the full force of the criminal law against someone who didn't have criminal intent, as in Morissette, is what rightly bothered him. It should bother us all.

Fifty years later, we see more criminalization of human error. Congress wrote the Clean Water Act to make it a crime to release pollutants into a river—regardless of the intent. Human error alone makes you a criminal. Parents who inadvertently leave a sleeping child in the car during the summer heat are brought up on criminal charges when that error leads to the child's death. Society clamors for it, if simply to have some reason to believe that by punishing this person, it somehow, magically, cannot then happen to us. Unfortunately, from a scientific perspective, these events are statistically predictable events and will randomly hit well-meaning people. Life is like the roulette wheel. For whoever is unlucky enough to make a mistake, to land on double zero, criminal charges are only an indictment away. It is but the most extreme version of Whack-a-Mole.

From corporate disciplinary policies to industry regulation to the criminal law itself—we have made human error a crime. It costs us in lives, it costs us in resources we could put to better use, it costs us any opportunity to learn how we might prevent or mitigate the next, inevitable human error.

PART FIVE

COMPENSATION

We try to learn. We take action with those who knowingly endanger other human beings. We design better systems, we help people make better choices. Yet, there is still that person who has already been harmed. What is the remedy for them?

Leaving the Garden of Eden

Remember Tommy and his volcano? Now that I think about it, perhaps Tommy would have been well served in creating two volcanoes. One for me to break and the other for display at the science fair. Call it insurance, if you will. It's part of planning for your own fallibility and the fallibility of those around you.

Such planning is what we're supposed to learn before we leave the safety net of our parents' nest. Part of that planning requires putting away a little money for a rainy day or the day when we are injured by some agent—that agent being ourselves, others, or acts of nature such as a lightning strike or hurricane. Life will deal us some lemons, so we need to be prepared.

Here, self-reliance is the objective. After all, we're all fallible human beings. I'm going to hurt a few people along the way, and I'll get hurt along the way. I'll pay for the injuries that occur to me, and you pay for the injuries that occur to you. Consider it the price for admission to the game of life. No need to whack each other…

OK. Most of us don't have the resources to set aside a

chunk of money for a new car after our car has been totaled by the driver who ran through the intersection; nor do we have excess cash saved for the accompanying medical bills and income loss. We would be wise to find another plan.

Enter: the World of Insurance

Insurance is ubiquitous today. It's everywhere—auto insurance, homeowner's insurance, travel insurance, long- and short-term disability insurance, unemployment insurance, general and professional liability insurance, health and life insurance. It seems that we can insure against just about any risk today, including risks to specific body parts. The singer Tom Jones reportedly insured his chest hair for $7 million; Tina Turner's legs are insured for $3.2 million; and rumors abound on the internet that Jennifer Lopez insures her bottom for anywhere from $32 million to a cool billion. Given that we all pose some risk of causing harm to others due to our inherent human fallibility, most of us now turn to insurance to prevent that harm from destroying our lives.

In modern life, insurance serves a good purpose. It is an opportunity to pool resources for the benefit of a collective group. Rather than requiring everyone to have cash reserves for any unanticipated future harm, we can pool our resources so that those combined resources can take care of the few who get injured. The system does not work very well when everyone in the pool gets injured, but works well when a small insurance premium paid by many can take care of the few who are injured.

So what risks are we insuring against? Is it harm caused by others? Natural disasters? Or is it harm caused by ourselves? The answer is all of the above. Imagine that we all carried first party insurance—that is, we carry insurance to take care of us in case of any future financial harm. Let's say 1,000 of my dearest neighbors form an insurance pool and each pays $1,000 a year into the fund. That's $1 million per year to spread among 1,000 in the pool who may be injured.

Let's say our neighbor, Bob, is struck by lightning; now he has $50,000 in unanticipated medical bills. Sally, she got in an automobile accident, injuring her neck; auto repairs and medical bills total $75,000. Fred's house burned down due to an electrical short in a coffee maker. That's $350,000. And Edna, she had a work injury, putting her out of work for six months. That's $35,000 in unearned income. And last, there was Billy, whose car was stolen right in front of his house. That's $30,000. So, at year-end, we'd have spent $540,000 to cover losses among the one thousand people in the insured group. At the end of the year, we'd add in the administrative costs, say $50,000, to create $590,000 in total costs. With $410,000 left over, we'd either refund the balance as a dividend, or we'd hold the remainder so that it would be available in future years. If we were all equally risk-prone, the system would seem perfectly fair.

Enter: the World of "Fault Finding"

Now, human nature being what it is, we might find a

few of our neighbors getting a bit greedy. They might say, "What if we sued the coffee maker for making a defective product? Could we recover $350,000 and increase the dividend we'd each receive? And, as an added bonus, we'd send a strong signal to the coffee maker manufacturers of the world that they'd better produce more perfect coffee makers."

And then there's Edna's work injury. Did the employer play a role in that injury? Could we sue Edna's employer to pay the bill, instead of our insurance fund?

And what about that Sally's auto accident? Did another driver cause the accident? Can we recover funds from him?

What about Billy's stolen car? Can we find the thief and recover money from him?

And finally, what about that lightning strike? Bob was at the golf course when he was hit. Did the golf course operator give Bob adequate notice of the impending storm? Was the golf course at fault? Was the Yahoo! weather report wrong? Heck, if the insurance group plays its cards right, they might recover all $540,000. Of course, in the process we would have hired insurance adjusters and bill collectors. Now transaction costs might have increased from $50,000 to $150,000. Oh, wait, there's also the lawyers we'd have to hire, better make those transaction costs $450,000 per year. Anyway, that $450,000 would be less costly than the original $540,000 we would have paid out. And, hey, perhaps we can invest that $550,000 we haven't used, say, in high yield home loans. Heck, with the right investments, our insurance fund can be a real moneymaker. Or, so we are led to believe.

Coming together as a collective group to pool everyone's risk exposure seems like an economically advantageous system and a positive contribution to the social good. Unfortunately, the bean counters seem to be in control. Rather than focusing on spreading the risk of catastrophe among a large group, the bean counters shifted the focus to minimizing payouts, recovering costs and maximizing profits for shareholders and corporate executives. They don't ask, "What is required to make this individual whole?" Instead they have shifted their energies toward finding out if someone in the group may have caused his or her own injury or loss—and if that's the case, then the group tries to shift blame onto the injured party. Did Billy leave his car unlocked or the keys inside his car, enticing the thief to steal the car? What about Edna—does she have a job that is too hazardous for the group? Perhaps that qualifies her for exclusion from the group completely! Or was Sally at fault in her automobile accident? Can the group now kick her out because, clearly, she's just not very careful?

If we know that good system design and behavioral choices can alter the rate of error, perhaps there's even more we could do. An investment on the front end, in designing safety systems, could reap additional rewards in reduction of adverse events. Perhaps that group could buy better, safer cars, or build houses with storm shelters, or gather together to create a neighborhood crime watch. There are thousands of things they could do to minimize the group's risks and minimize the payouts within the group. Indeed, the group of people who make better choices just might band together to create a different risk pool with lower contributions for safer people.

In that perfectly administered insurance risk pool, a Garden of Eden if you will, we'd all be working for the collective good. With similar systems and similar behavioral choices, the presence of an adverse event would only be a statistical result: unluckiness, if you will. The fact that it was Sally who got into the auto accident is not relevant. Next year it could be Edna or Billy. Sally's accident would be no indication of her blameworthiness or her intent toward the accident. In this idealistic insurance risk pool, Sally's accident would not cause us to re-evaluate the merits of keeping her in the risk pool.

However, in the real world, we face an almost limitless variety of system designs and behavioral choices. If Sally were intoxicated when the accident occurred, would it be just for the group to throw her out of the risk pool? Or, perhaps, we agree that reckless behavior should never be covered under the joint agreement in the first place?

That's the point of faultfinding, isn't it? Make those who "caused" the accident pay, so that they will take proper precaution to prevent future events. Without the incentive to avoid future payouts, why would any human being take precaution against future mistakes and mishaps?

Welcome to our civil liability system: a state-sponsored system for allocating blame and formulating remedies. This civil liability system in the U.S. currently serves two goals: restitution and deterrence. There are two dominant components of the system—contracts and torts. If you and I contract for the delivery of products or services, and one of us doesn't fulfill our end of the bargain, the court system can identify an appropriate remedy. That's contract law. The tort system, in parallel, supports the resolution of harm when there's no underlying contract. If you're injured in a car accident, the court affords an avenue for obtaining a remedy from the person who hit you.

The basic rule in our civil liability system is that if you make the mistake, you pay for it. It's the underlying tenet of American jurisprudence. It's not necessarily the central notion around the world, but in the U.S. it is foundational to our system of justice. The idea here is that if you've made a mistake, you're in the best position to change your own behaviors in order to prevent future errors. If you want to reduce payouts to others, society expects that you would design increasingly more reliable systems and make increasingly safer choices. That's the basic tenet of American accountability.

Stella Liebeck

Those of us who were adults in 1992 most likely heard of the story of Stella Liebeck, a 79-year-old woman from Albuquerque, New Mexico. On February 27, 1992, Liebeck's grandson ordered her a 49-cent cup of coffee in the drive-through at their local McDonald's. Liebeck's grandson parked the car so that she could add cream and sugar. Liebeck placed the cup between her legs, and in the process of taking the lid off, she spilled the entire cup of coffee on herself. According to court documents, she sat in the coffee for 90 seconds, scalding her thighs, buttocks, and groin. Liebeck suffered third-degree burns on six percent of her body, requiring skin grafts and an eight-day stay in the hospital. Liebeck sued McDonald's for producing a "defective" product. She argued that the coffee was "too hot." Liebeck claimed that McDonald's was "grossly negligent" (i.e., reckless) in selling unreasonably dangerous coffee. The rationale for the suit was that McDonald's coffee, served at 180 degrees Fahrenheit, could produce third-degree burns in only twelve to fifteen seconds. McDonald's, in turn, was trying to keep its coffee hot for the trip home or to the office. Given the fact that Liebeck was the one who spilled the coffee, making her partially "at-fault," the jury returned a verdict finding McDonald's 80 percent responsible for the accident, while holding Liebeck 20 percent responsible. The jury awarded $200,000 in compensation for the harm, and then awarded Liebeck $2.7 million in punitive damages. The judge in the case set aside the $2.7 million punitive damages award, reducing the punitive damages to $480,000.

This verdict, especially the $2.7 million in punitive damages, was definitely newsworthy and again sparked considerable public debate about the role and goals of the civil liability system. Other fast food restaurants and coffee shops were serving coffee at similarly hot temperatures, as they continue to do today. Standard coffee makers brew coffee at the same temperature with directions to serve immediately. Coffee is served hot—that's one of the things we like about it.

Yet whether Liebeck was harmed by her hand or by the hand of McDonald's, there was an injury to remedy. If you are a coffee brewer today, you simply live with potential lawsuits as a cost of doing business. Every year fast food restaurants and coffee houses are sued, some successfully, some not. For many plaintiff attorneys, the civil liability system is the defender of what is right—the tool of the individual to hold the big, bad corporation accountable for the harm it has caused. For others, Liebeck's case is about a civil liability system gone awry, where individuals are no longer accountable for their own actions. Somewhere in the middle is the truth or at least a position of justice that seems fair for the individual who was harmed. Somewhere in there, we would hope, is a means to designing a safer world for all of us. It's perhaps just a little hard to see.

Whack-a-Mole?

It's an expensive system, the American civil liability system. The Pacific Research Institute, a conservative California-based public policy institute, released a report in 2007 entitled, "Jackpot Justice: The True Cost of America's Tort System." This report estimated that the U.S. tort system costs approximately $865 billion each year—more per year than the hopefully once-in-a-lifetime bailout of the banking industry. They identified that 55 percent of these costs went to administrative costs and the lawyers on both sides of the fight. Only 45 percent went to the injured party. It was their estimate, of course questioned and criticized by everyone in the legal community, that the American tort system wastes $587 billion each year. I can make no claim to the accuracy of these numbers. I will leave that to the many commentators posturing around the excesses of our lawsuit-happy society. More fundamentally, what bothered me in the "Jackpot Justice" report is what it said about the objectives of the tort system itself:

> "Tort law has the goal of efficiently deterring wrongdoers and fully compensating unjustly injured victims."

Read these words carefully. Deterring wrongdoers. Fully compensating unjustly injured victims. Why do we call them wrongdoers? Why do we call them unjustly injured victims? Consider a basic traffic accident where one person inadvertently hits another. In this case, you've inadvertently run a red light and hit me. By definition, you are the "wrongdoer" and I am the "unjustly injured victim." Now, had you been intoxicated at the wheel of your car, I might rightly believe that you are a "wrongdoer." I would be angry at your drunken driving and believe that you should be deterred from that behavior again by any means necessary; I would expect to be made whole for the damages caused by your reckless choice. (Ideally, I would have preferred that you were caught driving drunk *before* you hit me, but that's a different discussion.)

Yet when such an accident occurs due to simple human

error, I think the label "wrongdoer" is too much. And the label "unjustly injured victim" is not right either. Because of our common fallibility, it's an unavoidable fact that we will all someday harm another human being. It's the roulette wheel—every day is a spin of the wheel, every day we face the fact that we may hurt another human being, or that we might be hurt. For those who work in a high-risk industry like healthcare, they will likely harm other people simply as a consequence of their career choice—likely to save many, yet also likely to injure a few.

What's Really Going On

There are two issues at play here. First is the effectiveness of the tort system in deterring undesired conduct. Was McDonald's sufficiently deterred by Stella's lawsuit? Do they and other coffee providers now sell coffee at a safer temperature? The answer, it seems, is "no;" your local Starbucks will gladly sell coffee at 180 degrees, the temperature of the coffee at which Stella was scalded, if requested. McDonald's continues to sell hot coffee—they've just made the warning on their cups quite clear:

CAUTION

Handle With Care

I'M HOT

The second issue is one of remedy. How should Liebeck take care of her injury? I do not believe that anyone is without sympathy for Liebeck's plight, an elderly woman painfully scalded over six percent of her body. But the lawsuit as remedy, the scale of the punitive damages, seemed both inefficient for making Stella whole (lawsuits typically take years to wind through the court system; the payouts, if any, often come too late to avoid financial hardship at minimum, or ruin at worst) and unfair to McDonald's. They were, after all, merely meeting consumer demand for hot coffee. The expense of the lawsuit and resulting financial damages seemed out of proportion to the event.

The unfortunate reality is that we are a lawsuit-happy society. We feel that it is our unalienable right as Americans to sue those who have done us wrong. Some of us might even think we have "scored" when someone makes a mistake and harms us. And along with that lawsuit is the public condemnation toward those being sued. They are "wrongdoers" out there hurting us, the "unjustly injured victims."

Whack-a-Mole.

Kiwi Compensation

Get into an automobile accident?
Exchange driver's license and insurance information with the
other driver.

Get injured at work?
Get medical attention and file a Workers' Compensation claim.

Injured playing intramural football?
File a claim with your health insurance company.

Hurt by your doctor?
File a medical malpractice lawsuit.

Spilt coffee causing third degree burns?
Sue McDonald's.

There are infinite ways you can get hurt—by your own hand, the hand of another, or just by natural disasters like tsunamis, hurricanes, and forest fires. In the U.S., each injury has its own potential remedy.

New Zealanders, or Kiwis as they're affectionately called, have a unique system for dealing with injuries. It's an approach that seems to better embrace the notion of human fallibility.

Sir Owen Woodhouse

His name is Sir Owen Woodhouse. He was a WWII torpedo boat commander for the New Zealand Navy. He was a lawyer trying automobile accident cases—as both plaintiff's counsel and defendant's counsel. He was eventually a New Zealand Supreme Court judge. Notable for our discussion is that he chaired a 1966 commission on personal injury in New Zealand. His report led to the creation of New Zealand's Accident Compensation Corporation (ACC). It is the only universal, 24-hour, personal-injury insurance scheme in the world.

Here is what Sir Owen Woodhouse had to say about the problem in 1967:

"One hundred thousand workers are injured in industrial accidents every year. By good fortune most escape with minor incapacities, but many are left with grievous personal problems. Directly or indirectly the cost to the nation for work injuries alone now approaches $50 million annually. This is not all. The same work force must face the grave risks of the road and elsewhere during the rest of every 24 hours. Newspapers up and down the country every day contain a bleak record of casualties."

Woodhouse saw that human beings have a propensity for injuring themselves and others. Helping New Zealanders with their injuries was Woodhouse's concern, not the labeling of one person a "wrongdoer" and one person an "unjustly injured victim."

Woodhouse was not impressed with our civil liability system in the U.S. He even referred to the "negligence action" (our U.S. tort system) as "a form of lottery." He saw those ways in which we could hurt each other, the ways we could all be victims, and the ways in which we could all be at fault. Suing each other, Sir Woodhouse claimed, was not the answer. He proposed an alternative scheme:

> "Immediate compensation *without proof of fault* for every injured person, *regardless of his or her fault*, and whether the accident occurred in the factory, on the highway, or in the home." [emphasis added]

Woodhouse went on to say that:

> "the adversary system hinders the rehabilitation of injured persons after an accident and can play no effective part beforehand in preventing them."

The accident compensation system in New Zealand is something that Americans should consider or, at the very least, take some lessons from. It's a system where, in the words of Woodhouse, "individual liability will disappear in favor of national responsibility."

Individual liability would disappear in favor of national responsibility—it is an extremely principled view. Woodhouse saw it as a matter of national responsibility to take care of those who were injured, whether at work, at home, or at play. He even saw that responsibility extending to visitors to New Zealand. So, the list of events that opened this chapter? It now looks like this:

Get into an automobile accident?

Get injured at work?

Injured playing intramural football?

Hurt by your doctor?

Call the Accident Compensation Corporation.

No wrongdoer. No unjustly injured victim. No lawsuit expenses. Only the commitment of New Zealanders to take care of one another when they are injured, regardless of the cause.

In the ACC scheme, finding appropriate restitution is a wholly separate activity from the task of deterrence. Deterrence is not lost in the New Zealand system— when it comes to drunk drivers, a first conviction can result in up to three months in jail. Additionally, look at their outcomes. Road accidents, work accidents, medical malpractice have rates similar to the U.S. and other industrialized countries. One would expect these rates to be significantly higher in New Zealand given the "deterrent" effect of civil lawsuits in the United States and other countries with similar civil liability systems. If one is convinced that accountability is lost in the New Zealand scheme, one would expect to find that injury rates increased after its adoption—why would anybody worry about harming others if they're not going to be held financially accountable? But accident rates have stayed consistent, suggesting, if anything, the intractability of human error.

The New Zealand system may seem unthinkable here in the U.S.—that we'd give up the right to sue in favor of collectively taking care of each other when someone is injured. For many of us, our right to sue is one of our God-given freedoms. Wrongdoers need to be taught a lesson. Unjustly injured victims need their day in court. Whack-a-Mole is in our blood and in our system of jurisprudence.

We do, however, have an example in the U.S. where we've given up our right to sue. Through our Workers' Compensation system, work injuries in the U.S. today are covered by a system similar to New Zealand's ACC. We learned long ago that having to sue our employer every time a workplace injury occurred would simply clog the courts with little overall efficiency. The court system is slow and costly. In an effort to get workers back on the job as quickly and as efficiently as possible, we created workers' compensation programs, where workers gave up their right to sue for a more certain injury benefit.

The New Zealand system is unique because it applies to all walks of life. New Zealanders call it 24-hour coverage. Whether you are injured at work, at home, at play, on the road, or in the hospital—you're covered.

It's something we should consider. The first target for change: medical malpractice in the U.S.

Retiring the Medical Malpractice System

Medical mishaps and healthcare-acquired infections cause an estimated 200,000 deaths every year in the U.S. alone. That's losing, *every year,* nearly 67 times the number of people lost in the September 11 terrorist attacks. Roughly 40 times the number of soldiers lost in Iraq and Afghanistan during the first seven years of warfare. Five times the number lost in automobile accidents. Each year. Almost 550 people every day, 1.8 million total since the IOM report was issued in 1999. That's the cost of medical mishaps and healthcare-acquired infections. Short of disease, it's the most likely cause of your own untimely death. In terms of national crises that lead to physical harm, it's at the top of the list, ahead of war, crime, suicide, and automobile accidents combined.

Perhaps you wonder why we're apparently all so sanguine about 200,000 preventable deaths each year—I know I do. Maybe it's because they happen one at a time? Losing fifty or 200 airline passengers in a single accident or thirty soldiers in one insurgent attack is so much more dramatic; these events always lead the evening news. But one person inadvertently killed at your local hospital? It rarely does. And so, that one individual's family is left to find their own way to wholeness. It is the medical malpractice system that offers hope, often on giant highway billboards put up by plaintiff attorneys: Hurt by your doctor? Call us!

What would the medical malpractice system look like here in the U.S. if we adopted the New Zealand approach? Answer: It would simply go away. We would retire it.

So what would this accomplish? Medical malpractice attorneys make two claims: 1) that the current system provides a needed remedy for those who are injured, and 2) that it deters future malpractice. Malpractice attorneys make the claim that injured parties rightly deserve some financial protection against the threat of unanticipated harm. I agree, and so do the New Zealanders. New Zealanders actually make the claim for all injuries, for whatever cause, not just those caused by healthcare misadventures.

Remember the report that said $587 billion is wasted in our U.S. tort system? In the area of medical malpractice, only 2.5 percent of injured patients even use the system. More than 97 percent of patients harmed by a medical mistake either never know their condition was caused by medical mistake, choose their own health insurance to provide the remedy, or they simply go without any meaningful redress. Rather than continuing with a system that is motivated to limit payouts, we could actually replace our current malpractice system with a no-fault system that would provide a remedy for all injuries received through the malpractice of a healthcare provider. As the New Zealanders say, we'll do it as a matter of national responsibility. And, by the way, the New Zealanders claim that their overhead expenses are only 8 percent as compared to administrative costs as high as 55 percent here in the U.S. And speed, well, four months to benefits in *contested* claims in New Zealand, whereas we average fifteen to twenty months to settle torts in the U.S. Oh, and one last thing, purely from a perspective of equity. An external review of the New Zealand system identified that only 5 percent of ACC claimants would have been able to prove fault in the American system. Ninety-five percent of claimants would have been without a remedy here in the U.S.

So what about the second claim, the deterrent effect of medical malpractice claims? The effect is simply not there—at least as a substantive tool for reducing what is now estimated at up to 200,000 lives lost per year in the U.S. There is no evidence that our tort liability system substantially changes individual behavioral choices of practitioners—particularly if what they're being sued for was a human error, by definition both unintentional and inadvertent.

Providers are apt to drift in their behavioral choices to places they believe are safe through personal experience, yet from a system-level perspective, appear risky. Take the CDC standards for hand hygiene, where rates of non-compliance among doctors are always lower than the compliance rate among nurses. It is generally the doctor, not the nurse, who gets sued for medical malpractice. Even with that increased threat of a lawsuit, doctors still lag behind in hand hygiene compliance rates.

In today's malpractice world, attorneys are forced to wait until there is injury before they reactively move in to punish the surgeon who we knew all along was engaging in risky behavioral choices. It is a totally reactive system, when the real system safety question should be, "How do we help the surgeon *before* his risky behavioral choices lead to harm?" How do we empower the state regulator and the local health care team to help the surgeon make better, safer choices before harm occurs? Given that we humans often disassociate our behavioral choices from their future unintended consequences, there is little hope that the tort system can help practitioners make substantially safer choices.

Build a Safer Healthcare System

Unfortunately, there is a lot of work to be done in our healthcare regulatory system. As we've seen, many healthcare regulators, including the Centers for Medicare and Medicaid Services and most state Departments of Health, are still playing Whack-a-Mole in their regulatory policies and approach.

We do need to provide a remedy for those injured by medical misadventure. We also need to build a safer healthcare system. Yet, our trust is simply misplaced when we believe that the medical malpractice system will help with a cure for either of these ills. The approach must be different, Whack-a-Mole has run its course; it has outlived its usefulness, if it ever had any.

Tossing the medical malpractice system will in itself not solve the problems we have. First, we'd have to replace it with a no-fault system of insurance, such as New Zealand's ACC or our own Workers' Compensation system. That would take care of the remedy for those who have been injured. Next, regulators and healthcare administrators would have to shift their focus from the severity of harm and who caused the injury, to the design of the healthcare system and the control of behavioral choices within the system. Our no harm, no foul system of accountability in healthcare today, turning a blind eye until harm occurs, must end. As a society, we need to shift to a more proactive system where system design and behavioral choices are additional measures of accountability—in healthcare, in automobile accidents, in spilt milk at the dinner table.

In healthcare, administrators and practitioners should be required to obtain basic competencies in safety science— especially around the roles of system design and personal behavioral choices. We must teach practitioners that they can influence the design of the system, and that in their behavioral choices they have some control over the likelihood of the undesired adverse event. Doctors and hospitals should be required to disclose adverse events and critical near misses, both to the patient and to the state. Transparency and accountability go hand-in-hand. What typically occurs in secrecy today, even between regulatory agencies within the same state, must be made visible.

Doctors and other individual providers must be required to participate in a more effective system of quality assurance that would involve near miss reporting, analysis, and corrective action. Many in the general public do not realize that hospitals have no real oversight over physicians; many physicians work as independent contractors and are given "privileges" at individual hospitals. If the physician/hospital relationship goes awry, the hospital's only recourse is often to rescind the doctor's privileges—something they are not motivated to do given the doctor's revenue-generating role. Practitioners cannot be allowed to work in isolation from a more formal system of quality assurance.

Most healthcare providers choose a life of service. They put themselves in harm's way to take care of others. They expect a lot of themselves as professionals. Yet, they remain fallible human beings, regardless of any oaths to do no harm. They are going to make mistakes and occasionally drift into risky places (see hand hygiene). The future of our nation's health depends upon our ability to learn from their errors and at-risk behaviors.

Policy makers, regulators, educators, administrators, and professional organizations must work to help change the public's perceptions about the appropriate accountability of healthcare providers. Accountability rests with practitioners' choices, not their errors or their unintended outcomes. This paradigm shift creates more accountability rather than less. There are alternatives to Whack-a-Mole—alternatives that have a history of success.

President Barack Obama has said that we need to re-evaluate our systems and toss those that do not work. I heartily agree. Medical malpractice, America's most sophisticated and expensive form of Whack-a-Mole, should be the first to go—if not merely to do the right thing for the professionals who dedicate their lives to the service of others, then for the millions injured and the 200,000 who are killed each year by a costly, ineffective healthcare system.

What Sports Can Teach Us

We can move away from the Whack-a-Mole game. We can change corporate disciplinary practices, we can change the way we regulate, and we can change our civil liability system. Ultimately, we can perhaps change the way we think about each other. Sports, strangely, might give us a glimmer of that change.

I must admit I've always had a bias against our cultural obsession with sports. I never quite saw what it taught us, and I certainly saw its downside. If it is between getting a good education and excelling in sports, our nation seems often to choose the latter. A look at the resources given to spelling bees and science fairs, compared to the resources given to football games? In many cases there is simply no comparison.

So, it pains me to suggest that the world of sports actually seems to be a model for accountability relating to our shared human fallibility. The differentiation between human error, at-risk behavior, and reckless behavior—and the notion that humans will not be perfect—is present in the world of sports. How we set up corporate disciplinary policies, how we set up our civil liability systems, how we should think about risk—they're all covered in sport.

A Sports Definition of Human Error

There are some experts in the study of human behavior who would loosely define human error as the failure of a human action to achieve the intended results. These experts would, when pressed, bring in some notion of inadvertency to their definition. Essentially, when a human's action produces an unintended result, we might label that action as a human error. I see the chocolate ice cream in the freezer, I reach in, pull out the tub of ice cream, and throw it into the grocery cart. I arrive home, unpack my grocery bags and find that I bought coffee-flavored ice cream instead. Same chocolate color, but entirely different words on the package. It's human error—inadvertent and unintentional.

When I was living in Minnesota, I had the opportunity, along with several thousand other spectators, to follow Tiger Woods around the golf course at one of the annual PGA championships. Imagine watching as Tiger plays golf. (I say "imagine" because the scenario that follows is wholly hypothetical). It's the final round, 18th hole. Tiger's down by two shots, 150 yards out from the hole and he knows he's got to put the golf ball in for a chance of forcing the playoff. It's a beautiful shot, landing just five feet above the pin on an upward slope. The ball lands and begins to roll backwards. We all roar as we see the ball head toward the hole. It looks on target, but as the ball approaches, it begins to nudge right, missing the hole by two to three inches. It settles to a stop just one foot from the hole—from a shot taken 150 yards away. Tiger knows now that his chances of winning the tournament are slim. He had fully intended to put the ball into the hole. It was his only goal, his only chance to win. Instead, he failed. The crowd, however, is still applauding wildly.

Now, did any of the spectators in the gallery see Tiger's failure as a human error? Did he make a mistake? Did he mess up? The scientist or engineer might say "yes," but most of us would say "no." Human error is not merely a failure to perform as desired. It also includes an element of social expectation. We expect Tiger to give it a shot, to try his best. Had he pulled out a 3 iron instead of his 9 and overshot the green by 100 yards, we might call that a significant error. Had he made the shot but written down the wrong score, causing a penalty and costing him the tournament, we might also call that an error. But we will not hang the label of human error around Tiger's neck for a shot from 150 yards away that misses the cup by only two or three inches.

Consider this scenario in our everyday expectations of those around us. Do we expect our physician to always get it right? Do we expect our dry cleaners to perform flawlessly? Do we expect our favorite restaurant to always deliver our meal exactly to our specifications? You might argue that sports are different, and that yes, we do expect our physician to always get it right. For a physician to make a mistake is just wrong, you might argue. The stakes are too high. While the sentiment is perhaps understandable and may serve to make us feel good about our tough stance, it's not the path to having the safest possible health care system.

Consider what makes a sport, a sport. You might say that it is not the "real thing" when compared to our jobs, or raising a child. It is meant to be play instead. You might also look at how we design a particular sport. We don't design sports so that participants get it right all of the time. To the contrary, we design games with the intent of causing human error. We design the game to produce a wide variation of human performance—so that the good players can excel against their peers. Natural talent, training, and attitude attempt to overcome the system designed with the express purpose of eliciting poor human performance.

The free throw line in basketball is 15 feet from the hoop. As a result, in the 2008 NBA season, only eight players made the free throw shot 90 percent of the time. The player ranked 73rd on this list made the shot less than 80 percent of the time. Some of the lesser shooters are in the 60 percent range. We easily could have put the free throw line three feet in front of the basket, greatly improving the average shooting percentage, but the game would likely lose some of its luster. There is a threshold, if you're Michael Jordan running to make an unchallenged layup, where failure to make the basket actually turns into human error. Short of that threshold, however difficult to define, we don't call it a mistake to fail to produce a desired outcome in sports. There's a time when a missed shot is simply a missed shot— no shame, no blame, no moral condemnation. Only a missed shot.

Justice in Sports

The system of justice in sports looks quite different from the corporate world. Look at intramural sports. When players make a mistake, like inadvertently running into another player on the field, we might very well begin thinking about justice and accountability. If we ran into another car on the road, we would clearly expect to give the other driver our insurance information. We pay for our own errors if they result in harm to another person. In sports, however, our expectations for justice work differently. If my buddy is not looking where he is running and inadvertently runs me over, spraining or breaking my ankle, I would not sue him for damages. My buddy would apologize and be there to help. I, the injured party, would take care of the injury and suffer the consequences of my inability to perform life's duties for the ensuing weeks while my ankle is in a cast.

The notion at play here is what lawyers call "assumption of risk." The idea is that we don't enter into the intramural sport without knowing that the sport is filled with risk. That risk comes from the inherent design of the game and the knowledge that we designed the game to promote human error. One of those errors might very well be the one that causes harm to another player.

Imagine you're in a bicycle race against 100 other bicyclists. You're out in front into the first turn, but you misjudge your ability to hold traction on the inside. You continue pedaling as you make the sharp turn, but your pedal hits the curb, causing you to tumble to the ground right in front of 99 other eager cyclists. As you fall to the ground, other cyclists attempt to steer around you, but with limited success. When the dust settles, 23 of the cyclists have fallen. Five of the bikes have significant damage; eight of the cyclists have injuries.

So what do we do? You made the error. Our everyday system of justice says that he who makes the error pays for its consequence. It's about deterrence, the lawyers tell us. So would we suggest that eight cyclists sue you to pay for the damage to their bodies? Would twenty-three cyclists sue you for the scratches to their bikes? Should they all file one big class action lawsuit?

Our answer is no. Unlike much of our other human endeavors that expect systems and the people within those systems to be perfect, sports comes with an assumption of risk. In the hypothetical bicycling accident, everyone will pay for the damage to his or her own bike or body. While the lawsuit might serve as a deterrent (although this is highly doubtful), the transaction costs (lawyers and investigators on both sides, the courts, judges, etc.) exceed any benefit received by allowing participants to sue each other for every error in sports that might lead to injury. It's the risk we assume in playing an organized sport or merely a pickup game of basketball at the local park. If we sued each other, arguing that justice would be served, we would simply clog the courts with little overall benefit—and miss out on a lot of fun.

Zidane's Head Butt

His name is Zinedine Zidane, one of the world's greatest soccer players. He wears golden shoes and produces golden outcomes. Midway through the finals of the 2006 World Cup between France and Italy, Zidane did the unimaginable. He walked up to an opposing player and headbutted the player in the chest. Premeditated, intentional, deliberate. It was no human error. The world watched, transfixed, as the star player on the French team seemingly lost his mind.

For an hour, players had fought it out on the field to maintain possession of the ball and score goals. Players ran into each other, players skidded into each other, players received penalties as part of the game—but it was all expected in this hard-fought battle to the world championship. But then, out of the blue, Zidane headbutted an opposing player. He was ejected from the game. Italy went on to win the game in the penalty shot playoff. Many soccer fans believe Zidane's exit cost France the game and four years of bragging rights to being the world's best soccer team. France is now forever the team with the player who headbutted another player. It will be indelibly written and preserved in the annals of sports history as one of the worst decisions ever made by a soccer player.

Zidane ultimately faced sanction from FIFA, the international regulating body for soccer. The question for the Italian player who was headbutted is whether the headbutt was one of the risks of playing that he had assumed in playing the sport? When we engage in sports, should we assume that another player might choose to intentionally harm us on the field? Do we not have a right to assume, even in professional athletics, that our opponents are not trying to hurt us outright (leaving boxing and mixed martial arts out of this argument for now)?

What if Zidane had broken the ribs of his victim or had hit his victim in a manner that led to the death of his opponent right there on the field? Do we merely assume it is a risk of playing the sport, or do we consider holding Zidane accountable for his choice to headbutt his opponent? In the law, in general, the concept of assumption of risk applies only to the human error or at-risk behavior. When your opponent acts with reckless disregard to the safety of you or your teammates, the law changes its view. The assumption of risk does not include the risk that other players will be reckless. Even in sports, there is a line we draw where the individual causing harm through reckless acts must pay for the damages.

We play pickup games of basketball at the local park with some expectation of the other players' court behavior. We expect that we'll all make mistakes and make stupid choices in the execution of our drive to the basket (the at-risk behavior). Beyond that, however, we should be able to expect that our fellow players will not choose to harm us, nor do we expect them to recklessly put us at unjustifiable risk. When they cross into that realm, we abandon the doctrine of assumption of risk and look squarely to the person engaged in reckless behavior to pay the bill, and to face sanction if we are in an organized league of some sort.

So, we're basically back to our earlier model—console the error, coach the at-risk behavior, punish the reckless behavior. And this is how it generally works at the pickup game. When our teammate misses a shot, we don't even think to console. We don't expect that we'll make every shot—how much fun would the game be if we did? When our teammate does make an error, such as passing the ball to a player on the other team, we might console them, "Hey, don't worry about it. It happens to us all." If our teammate chooses an at-risk behavior, like making errant passes behind the back, we might coach, "Hey, I think the behind-the-back passes are best left for the Harlem Globetrotters. We're trying to win the game!" Perhaps not so subtle, but it's coaching still the same. If our teammate engages in reckless behavior, like charging the basket, needlessly decking the opposing player, we might pull our teammate aside and impose a little corrective action. It might be that we eject him from the game. And if the other player gets significantly hurt, where there is obvious reckless behavior, the reckless player might legally become responsible for the harm.

It may seem strange to compare sports to being a commercial pilot or a doctor. They are more similar than we'd like to admit. In both, we ask individuals to perform as best they can. We design a system around them, and then we ask them to make the best possible behavioral choices they can within that system. In both the work world and in sports, we should expect human fallibility, human mistakes. In sports, we actually design the game to enhance that fallibility. The built-in, or enhanced, fallibility is what makes the game interesting. In medicine, we design the system to minimize that fallibility, but our fallibility remains.

We cannot and should not expect perfection from each other—no matter how critical the task may be. Our power is in the systems we build around imperfect human beings and in our expectations of them within those systems. A bad outcome should never automatically qualify a human being for blame and punishment. In the case of simple human error, there is no wrongdoer, there is no unjustly injured victim. There is only the predictable path that through our shared human fallibility we're someday going to hurt each other—whether at work, at home, or at play on the soccer field.

Perhaps sports can teach us all a thing or two about human fallibility and demonstrate to us all that there are alternatives to the game of Whack-a-Mole.

PART SIX

ONE PERSON AT A TIME

Yes, our whole society has embraced the game of Whack-a-Mole. Legislators, corporate executives, news reporters, managers, parents, individuals—we all fall prey to this addictive game. We can end the game, however, working one person at a time. In our work role, in our life as parents, in our reaction to the person who just ran into us on the road—we can make a difference, one person at a time.

Midlife Crisis, I Presume?

I ride motorcycles, both street and dirt bikes; I've been riding since I was a kid. I'm a "safety guy" and I ride motorcycles. In fact, on that first date with my wife-to-be (the date we were celebrating on that lovely September evening when the adverse drug reaction occurred), I asked her if I could pick her up on my motorcycle—she said no.

Motorcyclists are a different breed. They ride the roads virtually unprotected, especially if they're not wearing a helmet. It's an inherently risky endeavor. In 2006, nearly 5,000 people in the U.S. were killed while riding motorcycles. Approximately one in 1,000 registered motorcycles will be involved in a fatal collision each year. In spite of the risk, society allows motorcycling. Some states go so far as to approve motorcyclists not wearing helmets.

Imagine you're the mate of a 45-year-old male in the throes of a midlife crisis. Your husband wants a motorcycle. He needs a motorcycle. He's never ridden a motorcycle (or it's been twenty-five years since he's ridden). He wants to learn. He wants to avoid being one of those statistics. He wants to ride—but he wants to live.

Being the diligent and supportive mate that you are, you want to help. You poke around on the internet and discover that motorcycle fatalities have been on the rise for the last ten consecutive years. You discover further that it's not young whippersnappers dying on those crotch rockets; the rise is predominantly attributed to old codgers in midlife crises, buying bikes with engines that outsize their brains. Your mate, you note with alarm, is right in the middle of the at-risk population.

Your research also leads you to some eye-opening accident statistics. What do they say about why motorcyclists get into accidents?

Harry Hurt

Harry Hurt was an accident researcher at the University of Southern California who, in the late 1970s and early 1980s, conducted the first extensive research on motorcycle accidents. Here are eight of the fifty-five observations that Hurt and his research team made in their review of motorcycle accidents:

1. Approximately three-fourths of motorcycle accidents involved collision with another vehicle, which was most often a passenger automobile.
2. Approximately one-fourth of these motorcycle accidents were single vehicle accidents involving the motorcycle colliding with the roadway or some fixed object in the environment.

3. Vehicle failure accounted for less than 3% of motorcycle accidents, and most of those were single vehicle accidents where control was lost due to a puncture flat.

4. In single vehicle accidents, motorcycle rider error was present as the accident-precipitating factor in about two-thirds of the cases, with the typical error being a slide-out and fall due to over braking or running wide on a curve due to excess speed or under-cornering.

5. The failure of motorists to detect and recognize motorcycles in traffic is the predominating cause of motorcycle accidents. The driver of the other vehicle involved in collision with the motorcycle did not see the motorcycle before the collision, or did not see the motorcycle until too late to avoid the collision.

6. Deliberate hostile action by a motorist against a motorcycle rider is a rare accident cause...

7. Weather is not a factor in 98% of motorcycle accidents.

8. Intersections are the most likely place for the motorcycle accident, with the other vehicle violating the motorcycle right-of-way, and often violating traffic controls.

Armed with the data, you approach your husband for his first mandatory safety briefing:

"Honey, I've done some research to help you stay alive in this new, foolish chapter of your life. Here's what I've learned. First of all, if you get into an accident, don't blame it on the weather and don't blame your new bike. That's only 5 percent of accidents. It's most likely that another vehicle is going to hit you, and it will most likely be in an intersection. Given that, don't believe that the big Hummer intends to kill you; it's just not the case. Look out for stationary objects because there's some likelihood you're going to hit an object that wasn't even moving. And, oh by the way, don't drive at 205 mph—I read about that somewhere. In other words, be careful."

However well-intentioned, your well-researched safety briefing is not likely to be much help. Yet, it is often how we conduct safety briefings—in high-risk industries, and in our personal lives as parents and friends. Accidents are bad; don't get into an accident. It's sort of the proactive version of Whack-a-Mole: "Hey, moles are going to pop up, so don't be one of them, and above all, don't get hit by that hammer!"

To the credit of Hurt and his research team, Hurt's research was seminal in creating an understanding of the common threads of motorcycle accidents. To be helpful, however, a reader would have to convert these observations into concrete actions. It would have to be more than "be careful" or "motorcycling is dangerous." For inherently fallible humans, telling them to "pay attention" or "be careful" does nothing to address our inherent human fallibility. To be effective, a safety briefing must have two elements: recommendations for both system design changes and for changes in behavioral choices.

As hard as it may be for non-motorcyclists to believe, there is a very strong culture of safety in the motorcycling community. Yes, one might argue that the very act of riding a motorcycle is, *prima facie*, too risky to begin with, but after accepting the initial risk associated with motorcycle riding, cyclists regularly engage in discussions about safety. Contributing to that discussion, in August 2006 *Motorcyclist Magazine* wrote an article, "50 Ways to Save Your Life," representing the collective wisdom of its editorial staff. Fifty ways to keep safe on a motorcycle? As an avid cyclist and safety guy, I had to read it.

Here's what I found. The list, quite different from Hurt's observations, doesn't tell me under what circumstances I am likely to die on a bike, nor is it merely a list of warnings for me to be careful. Some suggestions are more tangible than others. For the sake of clarity, I've reworked the list based upon whether the rules relate to system design or in-the-moment behavioral choices. Here are some of their recommendations that should be applied prior to riding:

3. and 38. Wear the right gear.

27. Don't take too much with you.

32. Master the slow U-turn.

39. Leave the iPod at home.

40. Learn to swerve.

44. Train your peripheral vision.

46. Carry a clear face shield.
48. Learn to use the front brake.
49. Check your tires.

These are the elements of system design that can (and should) be addressed by the motorcyclist prior to riding. A few relate to equipment (e.g., right gear), and a few to building proficiency (e.g., using the front brake). There are, of course, a number of items relevant to the quality of the bike, (tires, braking systems), additional safety equipment (protective riding gear), and the training of the rider. These are the system design elements, pre-riding, that the *Motorcyclist* staff saw as the most important for increased riding safety.

The bulk of the safety recommendations, however, addressed behavioral choices during the ride. According to the *Motorcyclist* staff, these include:

2. Don't cut off the bad driver.
7. Turn your head to see before changing lanes.
8. Take a timeout before passing or pulling away from a curb.
9. Do not approach parked cars or change lanes at high speed relative to the cars you are passing.
10. Scan the sides of roads for troublesome debris.
12. Look both ways after the light changes.
13. Check your mirrors before changing lanes, slowing down, or stopping.
14. Put one second of distance per 10 mph between you

and the vehicle in front of you.

16. Enter curves and corners at slow speeds.
17. Slow down when you're in an animal-rich area.
18. Use both brakes.
19. Keep the front brake covered—always.
20. Look where you want to go.
21. Keep your eyes moving.
23. Look ahead, not right in front of the bike.
25. Come to a full stop at that next stop sign.
26. Never dive into a gap in stalled traffic.
31. Give your eyes some time to adjust in varying light levels.
33. Use the rear brake to prevent rolling back on a hill.
35. Ease back on throttle, brake gingerly when tire blows.
37. Don't ride if you are mad, sad, exhausted, or anxious.
41. Use rear brake to smooth low-speed maneuvers.
42. Tap your brakes before stopping.
43. Put a vehicle between you and traffic coming through the intersection on the right.
45. Use kickstand to trip light.
47. Don't sit next to—or right behind—large trucks.

Every recommendation in the list above relates to behavioral choices I can make while riding. As we should all recognize by now, this does not mean that I should expect I'll be perfect—because I won't be—but these are tangible behaviors that I should engage in to ensure that I arrive safely home to my wife and kids.

The list of fifty safety recommendations also contained some recommendations that were not obvious system design elements or tangible behavioral choices. For this reason, they are not as immediately valuable as the preceding lists. They certainly put riders on notice, but without requiring riders to make some strong inferences, the recommendations do not directly let them know the system design or behavioral choice element that will reduce the risk of an accident. These less helpful recommendations are:

22. Think before you act.
28. Watch for car doors opening in traffic.
29. Don't get in an intersection rut.
34. If it looks slippery, assume it is.
36. Pay more attention when the road is wet.
50. Take a deep breath.

The differences are subtle—leaving the iPod at home is a concrete recommendation. Tapping the brakes to alert the car behind you that you intend to stop is a concrete behavioral recommendation. Applying maximum level concentration and caution when driving in the rain—well, that's a bit like warning me not to make a mistake. What is it that you want me to do differently when I'm riding in the rain?

Motorcyclist Magazine did a good job in making actionable system design and behavioral recommendations. The motorcycle community recognizes that riders are fallible, and it definitely stresses that other drivers are prone to making mistakes. Expectations of perfection, while prevalent in the healthcare and aviation industries, are not at all evident in the motorcycling community. Rather, the motorcycle community simply wants the motorcyclist to survive the many mistakes they and other drivers are going to make. And, for the most part, it recognizes that good system design, and good behavioral choices will be the key to safer outcomes.

System design and behavioral choices—the two things we have control over as we make our way through the world. Rather than telling me to be careful, my wife can offer up this nugget, "Don't forget to cover your front brake." Rather than telling my three-year-old son to be careful with his milk, I can teach him to always place the milk toward the center of the table—or if I really want to be spill proof, I can put the milk in a sippy cup. Rather than tell my employee to be careful, I can give them a checklist for the task at hand. Rather than telling myself to remember to bring that critical report to work tomorrow, I can choose to get out of bed and put the report in my computer bag, or even better, take it to my car—even if it does require getting out of bed right in the middle of the *Colbert Report*!

I recently went to an ice cream store with part of my family. Some of the kids were at home. We called, asked them if we could bring home some ice cream. We stood in line, ordered our ice cream cones along with two pints to take home. Not wanting those two pints to melt while we ate our ice cream in the shop, the ice cream scooper offered to put them into the freezer behind the counter. Good idea. When I paid, she handed me an empty bag and said, "So you don't forget." I quickly asked, "So do a lot of people forget?" "Yes," she said, "they do."

She could have just as easily reminded me upon paying to not forget about the two pints in the freezer, but she did more. She designed a system that significantly decreased the likelihood that I would leave without remembering my two pints to take home. She designed a better system. While we ate our ice cream in the store, we all sat looking at that empty folded bag. I was impressed with this simple, yet elegant solution.

Non-actionable advice—be careful, pay attention, don't get into an accident—these statements do little to improve outcomes. You might as well say, "Be perfect." We must do more to help each other—in the design of systems and in reinforcing good behavioral choices.

One last note on New Zealanders. Motorcyclists during their first year of motorcycling, regardless of age, are required to drive a motorcycle with an engine size of 250cc or less. The Kiwis understand that big engines and midlife crises don't mix. Here in the U.S., well, it's survival of the fittest.

Spilt Milk

Yes, I'm a parent. Five children.

It would be hard to write a book about error and justice without talking about the training ground for who we are today. Much of our training came early, by watching our parents' reactions when we made mistakes or engaged in at-risk or reckless behaviors.

As parents, we struggle to find the right system of accountability, particularly in the punishment we hand down. Do we spank? Do we put our children in time out? Do we restrict their activities, take away something they love? There are hundreds of books and thousands of experts with opinions on what constitutes appropriate disciplinary action for a child. To that debate I can add very little.

Instead, I want to turn toward the underlying substantive basis for disciplinary action in the first place. What do we teach our children about their own fallibility when we punish them? What expectations do we set? How do we judge the spilt milk? While my children would attest to the many instances where I've failed as a parent in my responses to their behavior (as they say, parenting isn't for cowards), I do have a guide. I know when to console, I know when to coach, and I know when to consider a more penalty-driven approach.

Consider 10-year-olds. At that age, some of their duties fall under the duty to produce an outcome: cleaning the bedroom, taking a shower, brushing teeth. These are duties where, by the age of 10, a child should have the ability to produce the result with little guidance. The parent sets the expectation, and the child produces the outcome—we do not need to show them how, nor should we help in the process. These are standard parental expectations, much like the code of conduct within the corporate world. These duties are the basic building blocks of personal hygiene, and accountability falls squarely on the child.

You can imagine a conversation with your child going something like this:

> Your job is to have your room clean for inspection by noon on Saturday. I don't care how or when you do it. I will simply inspect the room. If it's not clean, you lose [insert highly-valued object or activity] for the day. Should you not meet the expectation, I'll inspect again tomorrow at noon. If it's not clean, you'll lose the privilege again.

This scenario is similar to the burger joint discussed earlier, the one where they can't give me my cheeseburger with a tomato but without lettuce. As parents, we're like the customer. We set the expectation, and our kids try to meet that expectation. If they get it wrong, we're not the ones to investigate—they are. We take no shared accountability for the breach (as we might when inspecting the bedroom of a four-year-old). It's up to our children to design the system and to make the right behavioral choices.

Will they produce perfect outcomes? No. They will typically miss some required items—picking up *all* the toys, putting all their dirty clothes in the hamper, wiping down the sink *and* the counter. Sometimes, they may fail to produce the outcome at all (they get distracted by a neighborhood football game or by a new computer game, or they just rebel to test the boundaries). The reasonable parent will set an expected rate of success depending on the task's difficulty and any risks associated with the failure to produce the outcome (leaving toys out isn't as risky as leaving wet, molding clothes on the carpet).

One option is to tell our children that they get one pass each year, or once a month depending on your tolerance level. That is, they get one opportunity to fail that does not lead to any sanction. Additionally, parents might give a pass for circumstances out of their control, such as Aunt Martha's untimely death or Dad's auto accident that derailed everyone's schedule for the week. Every responsibility should be met with a reasonable expectation.

Now, beyond the basics—bedroom cleaned, teeth brushed, garbage emptied—there is the rest of life with all its complexity. Our children face a number of overlapping values, a plethora of duties, and a seemingly unending list of individual tasks. Life is complex, even for a 10-year-old. We advise our kids that they are going to make mistakes in life now and through their last dying days. They will never be immune from human error. The important thing is that they be honest when they do make mistakes. As parents we try to create an environment where our children can talk with us about their mistakes, without much fear that they will be disciplined for coming forward with their error. Just as an airline or a hospital needs a strong reporting culture to see the precursors to future, much more catastrophic events, our homes need a strong reporting culture as well. Our children need to feel safe to report their errors so that we can help them learn from their mistakes. Rather than punish for the spilt milk, we should console around the error. Rather than punish because of the muddy footprints on our newly installed crème carpet, we should coach around the at-risk behavior of wearing their shoes inside the house. When we do this, we lay the groundwork for trust, for keeping the dialogue open during the teen years, when we really need our teenagers to come forward about their at-risk and even reckless behaviors.

Now, you might ask, what is our role in parenting when every time our kid makes a mistake, we are consoling? Don't worry—kids, like adults, engage in a lot of at-risk and reckless behavior—there will be plenty of opportunity for coaching and punishing!

Children engage in a lot of at-risk behaviors. As adults, we seem to choose the at-risk path because we feel the pressure of too many things to do, and we under-appreciate or undervalue the risks that we are taking—smoking, speeding, gossiping. For younger children, many at-risk behaviors occur because they simply don't have the experience to know that what they're doing is risky. The child who places his milk glass right at the edge of the table lacks the experience to recognize this as risky—whereas, the parent, with ample experience cleaning up spilt milk immediately recognizes the risk. For our children who are just trying to sit down for dinner and enjoy the company of their siblings or friends and keep track of the cartoon playing on the TV, milk safety is the furthest thing from their minds. So, we coach them.

Dad: Sally, you should really put your glass of milk behind your plate, closer to the center of the table. It takes only one mistake, turning to talk to your brother, not seeing your elbow swing, and you've knocked over the glass of milk.
Sally: Sure, Daddy.

OK, that's ideal. Not necessarily how it goes in every instance, but it's the goal.

In practice, perhaps after a long day at the office, the exchange looks more like this:

Dad: Sally. Sally! Yoo hoo, Sally! How many times have I told you to put that milk glass behind your plate? Just how many times? Do you have a brain inside that head of yours? I'm getting tired of telling you. Perhaps losing the privilege to play with your friends for the rest of your life would get you to pay better attention. Move that milk right now!

Sally, dejected: Sure, Daddy.

Coaching is tough. An at-risk behavior has been identified and just this mere fact causes stress levels to rise. In the parental context—perhaps in most contexts—coaching can easily degrade into yelling or something that feels like yelling to the recipient. Coaching turns from a positive, teachable moment to punishment. As parents, we often reach a heightened level of frustration when our kids are not responsive to our initial coaching efforts. We may go so far as to get our children's hearing tested because they seem so unresponsive!

But think about your own receptivity to coaching. Do you respond immediately to that one police officer who writes a warning instead of a ticket for speeding? Coaching makes sense intellectually, but actually changing our behaviors in response to coaching is much more complex. In theory, our child could draw a map of where the milk should be positioned on the kitchen table based on household policy. And they could practice proper glass placement over and over until they get it right. In reality, sitting down to dinner is a much more robust activity. There's a flurry of activity with setting the table and getting the meal on the table while it's still hot. We're concerned about what's for dinner tonight and whether we like it, we're telling a story to a sibling or our mates; if we're a teenager, we're listening to our iPods or texting a friend so as to ignore his boring family. The last thing anyone is concerned with is the proper positioning of the milk glass.

Coaching is an ongoing life activity. It's what we owe our children. It's what we owe each other. For our children, it should be in a loving fashion, both in our choice of words and in our tone. Now, if our children remain unresponsive to a particular line of coaching, we can turn to what employers call counseling. That is, let our children know that disciplinary sanction is coming their way if they do not begin to make different behavioral choices.

Then, of course, there's the day that you walk in the kitchen and find your 10-year-old winging a fork across the room, right at the face of his pesky 16-year-old brother. The fork narrowly misses the 16-year-old's head. The 10-year-old sees it in your eyes; he's busted. So, in a desperate attempt to get out of this mess, he yells, "But Dad, I missed." It is at this point your accountability compass is tested. Was throwing the fork at his brother's face a reckless act? Or did the 10-year-old have a point? After all, no one got hurt. No harm, no foul? The answer is no. It's not no harm, no foul. It is reckless behavior, and that's what you tell him. It's about the quality of his choices, and that it's in his choices that he has control—and in his last choice he was reckless toward the safety of his big brother.

Parenting *isn't* for cowards. And while we live and work in a society with a whacked sense of accountability, as parents, we have the opportunity to change the world. We can teach our children about human fallibility by not expecting perfection from them and by teaching them not to expect it from themselves. We must demonstrate to our children that human errors are different from at-risk or reckless choices. We must teach them that it's the behavior that counts, and that they cannot walk perilously close to the edge of a cliff without eventually falling off. Their behavioral choices will dictate the likelihood of future harm—to themselves or others. Whack-a-Mole and no harm, no foul are no more effective as parenting strategies than they are as business strategies. It simply teaches our children to divorce their behavioral choices from the harmful events that may or may not result.

You

None of us had any choice in whether we were born or not. Unlike in sports, none of us had a choice in signing life's "assumption of risk" waiver. The simple act of our birth is an assumption of risk. And as we've seen throughout this book, life is filled with risk.

For more than twenty years I've been working in high-consequence industries, trying to help *them* reduce the likelihood of inadvertently killing *you*. I'm clearly not alone in that endeavor. Thousands of safety officers, systems engineers, risk management groups, human factors specialists, to name a few, have and are working this task. With that said, there is more work to do.

What have I learned during the past two decades? Two key observations that form the foundation for this book: first, we want each other to be accountable. We create social systems that allow us as a group to go after those who cross societal lines—from tort law, contract law, criminal law, and administrative law to the dreaded homeowners' association. As a society, we cast a net as the fisherman does and catch those who are not conforming.

The problem is that the net has been cast too wide, often unjustly classifying mere human mistakes as criminal actions. Yes, the criminal law is perfectly applicable in cases where a person purposefully harms or recklessly endangers others. The problem is with inadvertent, unintentional human errors. We've lumped the doctor who makes the inadvertent error in with the doctor who anesthetizes his patient in order to have sex with her. Our society sees injustice in both—where one is truly unjust, but the other is simply the predictable side effect of our human existence. Somewhere along the way, we've lost the practical differentiation between human error, at-risk, and reckless behaviors. In doing so, we've created only one standard: perfection.

Second, when something does go wrong, the only thing society focuses on is the actual negative outcome—we de-emphasize the roles of system design and behavior. We embrace a no harm, no foul philosophy to the point that we condone or even facilitate reckless choices as long as no adverse event has occurred. The U.S. banking crisis should be a glaring example of that. It's all good. Look at my rising house value, look at my rising stock value. Wait, wait— what's happening? Why's the bottom falling out? This isn't supposed to happen! Who's responsible for this? Wall Street bankers, those guys getting those huge bonuses? Yep, it's them. "Off with their heads," we say. We hypocritically demonize the Wall Street bankers and ignore our own complicity—we turned a blind eye as long as our stock and home investments were on the rise. See no evil, hear no evil, speak no evil—until the mole pops up out of his hole. Then whack him and assume all is again right with the world.

I've been helping to re-work this no harm, no foul approach to managing risk for decades now, suggesting different ideas about accountability to corporate managers, regulatory authorities, and everyone in between. There comes a point, however, where social change cannot further progress until the concepts are placed in front of the entire marketplace of ideas. And that leads me to you. You can make the difference. You can take the next step.

You can make a difference not only in your own life, but in the lives of your children, friends, and co-workers. You can make a difference in the event an airline, restaurant, hobby shop, or hospital inadvertently harms you, whether physically or financially. The power is in your hands. Legislators are steeped in the game of Whack-a-Mole. They will be unwilling to change the game until we the people demand the change. How?

Saving Yourself

First, own your personal fallibility. Don't believe that you are above being an inherently fallible human being. You can't will yourself to perfection. Know that when an error hits you, it's not necessarily an indication of bad behavior. You are not a wrongdoer worthy of public condemnation and sanction simply because you made a mistake.

Second, know that you have choices to make. Choices about the system you design around yourself. Choices to make within that system—from drinking and driving, to relying heavily on your faulty memory. Our choices will determine the risks we impose on others, and it is for our choices that society can rightly stand in judgment. Third, don't let the severity bias lull you. Just because you had a good outcome doesn't mean your risky choice ought to be validated. Step back, search your mind and your soul: am I doing the right thing? No harm, no foul cannot be a guiding principal of life. Remember, each day is a spin of the roulette wheel—saving ourselves and saving others means we try every day to maximize the number of spaces through good system design and good behavioral choices. Just because we didn't land on double zero today does not mean that the double zero isn't there.

Judging Others

Now, be fair, be just with others. Think twice about how you judge the restaurant that messes up your order, the driver who cuts you off, and the doctor who orders the wrong medication. We should not be suing each other every time another person makes a mistake that harms us. The costs are simply too high. I need to accept that my healthcare provider, my airline pilot, my neighbor, my mate, and my children are fallible. Just as tornados and lightning strikes are unavoidable, predictable components of the weather, I know that human fallibility, my own included, is an unavoidable, predictable component of being human. When mistakes occur and harm results, we should give aide to those who are harmed and act with compassion toward the person who made the mistake.

We have it within our control to build a safer, more compassionate society. While we can't expect perfection, we can hold each other accountable for the quality of our choices. At the end of the day, that is all we can do. I must live with your fallibility, you must live with mine. To ask for more—well, that only leads in one direction.

Whack-a-Mole.

NOTES

Prologue

Throughout *Whack-a-Mole* there is reference to Dr. Lucian Leape's testimony before Congress and his co-authorship of the Institute of Medicine (IOM) report "To Err is Human," published by National Academy Press (2000). For further reading, a transcript of his testimony can be found online through the American Psychological Association's website, <www.apa.org/ppo/issues/sleape.html>. For an easy-to-read overview of worldwide injury statistics, you can refer to Peden M, McGee K, Sharma G. The injury chart book: a graphical overview of the global burden of injuries. Geneva, World Health Organization, 2002.

Spinning the Roulette Wheel

The entire Presidential Commission on the space shuttle *Challenger* accident, also known as the Rogers Report, can be found online at history.nasa.gov/rogersrep.

The Encyclopædia Britannica entry for Christa McAuliffe (accessed Feb. 12, 2009) can be found at <http://www.britannica.com/EBchecked/topic/353747/Christa-Corrigan-McAuliffe>.

To Err is Human

Information on parents who forget their children in the car and the effect of ambient temperatures can be found in "Heat Stress From Enclosed Vehicles: Moderate Ambient Temperatures Cause Significant Temperature Rise in Enclosed Vehicles." Published by Pediatrics (2005). An online version of this article can be found at <www.pediatrics.org/cgi/content/full/116/1/e109>. National statistics are available at <http://ggweather.com/heat/>.

The Statistical Summary of Commercial Jet Airplane Accidents 1959-2007 is available online at <www.boeing.com/news/techissues/pdf/statsum.pdf>.

For further reading on aircraft accidents caused by human error, take a look at "A Human Error Analysis of Commercial Aviation Accidents Using the Human Factors Analysis and Classification." Published by the U.S. Department of Transportation (2001).

The National Transportation Safety Board publishes aviation accident statistics online at <http://www.ntsb.gov/aviation/Table6.htm>.

Ignaz Semmelweis

A veritable catalyst for change, Ignaz Semmelweis has numerous books and articles written on his hand-washing "phenomenon." The 2009 Encyclopedia Britannica Online offers a nice overview at <http://www.britannica.com/EBchecked/topic/534198/Ignaz-Philipp-Semmelweis>. Sherwin B. Nuland also wrote on Semmelweis's discoveries in "The Doctors' Plague: Germs, Childbed Fever, and the Strange Story of Ignac Semmelweis." Published by W. W. Norton & Company (2003). The Center for Disease Control first released its study on hospital-acquired infections in 2002. (Over the years, there has been a shift in terminology to refer to hospital-acquired infection as healthcare-acquired infections.) A summary of its findings can be found at <http://www.cdc.gov/od/oc/media/pressrel/r021025.htm>. The U.S. National Center for Health Statistics offers valuable data on the country's leading causes of death. Visit <http://www.cdc.gov/nchs/FASTATS/lcod.htm> for more information.

205 Tilley

Sam Tilley's speeding ticket garnered national attention from most of the country's top newspapers, including *USA Today* <www.usatoday.com/news/offbeat/2004-09-21-speeder_x.htm>. In the motorcycle community, there is debate about whether or not Tilley's motorcycle could even reach 205 mph—blog sites abound and offer humorous and occasionally informative perspectives. For interested readers, the actual speeding ticket can be viewed at <www.thesmokinggun.com/archive/0922042speed1.html>.

100,000 Pages

The Aviation Safety Network has published a comprehensive overview of the American Airlines Flight 191 crash at <http://aviationsafety.net/database/record.php?id=19790525-2>. A link to the entire NTSB accident report can also be found on the same site.

Doing the Right Thing

Adding to the many side stories within the *Titanic* tragedy is the conflicting evidence around J. Bruce Ismay. Though initial press reports labeled him as the main force behind the *Titanic*'s unsafe speeds, mail correspondence before the ship's sailing seems to indicate otherwise—

Ismay's tone in these letters conveys Ismay's wariness in causing such a large ship to arrive in the harbor ahead of schedule. These letters and more can be found at <www.titanichistoricalsociety.org/articles/ismay.asp>.

The initial investigation and subsequent report that was commissioned after the *Titanic*'s sinking, "Loss of the Steamship 'Titanic'" can be accessed online through Google books.

Information on the key that kept the *Titanic*'s crow's nest binoculars locked away can be found at <http://www.telegraph.co.uk/news/uknews/1561604/key-that-could-have-saved-the-titanic.html>.

No One to Help

Kitty Genovese's murder is curious not only for the resulting nationwide study of the "Genovese syndrome," but also for its contested facts. In subsequent investigations, it turns out that based on the size of the trees outside of Genovese's apartment and the light emitted by a lamppost, her neighbors' view of the street was quite constricted. The thirty-eight people who were reported by the *New York Times* as "witnessing" her attack have never been verified. In actuality, there could have been maybe one or two who saw her, but based on their testimony, Genovese would have been alone and stumbling from her attack as though she were simply walking home from one of several local bars.

The original *New York Times* article written by Martin Gansberg in 1964 can be found through a web search or via the *Times*' online archives. Though there are many comprehensive sites that discuss the case's disputed facts, one that I found most intriguing was <http://kewgardenshistory.com/ss-nytimes-3.html>. *Times* reporter Jim Rasenberger wrote an excellent article on Genovese on the fortieth anniversary of her murder, "Kitty, 40 Years Later," which is available at <http://query.nytimes.com/gst/fullpage.html?res=9A03E1DF1E3BF93BA35751C0A9629C8B63>.

Christopher Sercye's death made national news and quickly infiltrated the topic boards of blogs. The *New York Times* article can be found here: <http://query.nytimes.com/gst/fullpage.html?sec=health&res=9A05EED6163CF931A35756C0A9659C8B63>. The EMTALA law that was enacted as a result of Sercye's death can be reviewed at <www.emtala.com/law>.

A Complicated Mess?

As gruesome as the numbers may be, the National Highway Traffic Safety Administration provides a very valuable learning tool for the public. Reports on traffic injuries, fatalities, etc. can be found at <www.nhtsa.gov>.

The state of Wisconsin's "OWI and Related Alcohol and Drug Penalties (As of 2007 Act 226; May 30, 2008)" can be accessed at <www.dot.wisconsin.gov/safety>.

State Whacking

Commercial aviation's accident rates can be found in Boeing's "Statistical Summary of Commercial Jet Airplane Accidents: Worldwide Operations 1959-2007." (Published by Boeing Commercial Airplanes: 2008.)

To learn more about the Aviation Safety Reporting System, visit <http://www.faa.gov/safety/programs_initiatives/aircraft_aviation/asap/>.

The NTSB law judge's comments can be found in Engen v. Chambers and Lansford: 1986 WL 82575 (N.T.S.B.).

Healthcare Whack-a-Mole

For those interested in reading a full version of Washington State's RCW 18.130.180, it can be found at <http://apps.leg.wa.gov/rcw/default.aspx?cite=18.130.180>.

How About Making It a Crime?

The criminal prosecution of Joseph Lepore and Jan Paladino is only one of many national Whack-a-Mole examples. The *Washington Post's* article is a good place to start: <http://www.washingtonpost.com/wp-dyn/content/article/2006/12/08/AR2006120800835.html>.

Julie Thao's criminal complaint can be accessed online at <http://www.wha.org/legalAndRegulatory/thao_bailmemo.pdf>.

The case documents for Morissette v. United States, 342 U.S. 246 can be found online via <lp.findlaw.com>.

Leaving the Garden of Eden

A great place to start is with *New York Times* reporter Dan Shaw's article, "Coffee, Tea Or Ouch?" It can be found online at

<http://query.nytimes.com/gst/fullpage.html?sec=health&res=9C0CE6 DE163CF931A25753C1A962958260>.

In a little more than fifty pages, "Jackpot Justice: The True Cost of America's Tort System" addresses the increasingly complex and costly tort system. Published by Pacific Research Institute (2007).

Kiwi Compensation

Sir Owen Woodhouse's "Compensation For Personal Injury in New Zealand: Report of the Royal Commission of Inquiry" (1967) is available online through The University of Auckland <http://www.library. auckland.ac.nz/data/woodhouse/> and offers a chance to read Woodhouse's original verbiage and ideas on the Accident Compensation Corporation.

Retiring the Medical Malpractice System

The 2008 annual report, "Accident Compensation Corporation in New Zealand," reports on the economic and social effectiveness of the ACC. An electronic version of the ACC's annual report can be found at <www.acc.co.nz>.

Current data on soldier casualties in Iraq and Afghanistan can be found at <icasualties.org>.

Midlife Crisis, I Presume?

Harry Hurt is known as the godfather of motorcycle accident research; a summary of his "Motorcycle Accident Cause Factors and Identification of Countermeasures" (published by the University of Southern California in 1981) can be found at <www.ct.gov/dot/LIB/dot/ Documents/dhighwaysafety/CTDOT_Hurt.pdf>. The entire document is available for purchase through the National Technical Information Service <http://www.ntis.gov/>.

Special thanks to *Motorcyclist Magazine* for allowing me to work with its "50 Ways to Save Your Life," which can be found at <http://www.motorcyclistonline.com/howto/122_0608_50_ways/index. html>.

ACKNOWLEDGEMENTS

I have been on this specific journey for more than fifteen years. There are many to thank.

I'd like to first thank the team at By Your Side Studios: Dave Wise, publisher; Amanda Bray, Literary Arts; and Shaun Zokaie, Graphic Arts. Also, I'd like to thank our reviewers; your valuable time in reading the manuscript and offering editorial comments is greatly appreciated.

I have had many mentors. My individual bosses played a great role in the path that led to Whack-a-Mole: Earl Robinson, Scott Bradbury, Peter Ansdell, Curt Graeber, and Dave Nakata. My colleagues at Outcome Engenuity, past and present, have been particularly influential—I thank you for your patience in the long journey to create this book.

To my colleagues in the industry, for those we at Outcome Engenuity have worked to serve, I owe a great debt. Without your embrace, we could have hardly shown the world there was a better path. While the list is long, notable steps on the Just Culture journey have been taken by the Civil Aviation Authority of New Zealand, the Minnesota Alliance for Patient Safety, the North Carolina Board of Nursing, the North Carolina Center for Hospital Quality and Patient Safety, the Missouri Center for Patient Safety, the California Patient Safety Action Coalition, and the U.S. Agency for Healthcare Research and Quality. In addition to coalitions, there are a great many individual organizations that have embraced this movement, making these concepts work at a very practical level.

Lastly, I'd like to thank my dear colleagues who were

my research partners—challenging my ideas, guiding my path: Scott Griffith, John Westphal, Sharon Comden, and Marie Dotseth, and my own Alex P. Keaton, my eldest son, Aaron.

And of course, my co-author/editor, wife, and best friend, Dawne Marx.

INDEX